To Murray
love from Janie
Christmas '82.

A Portrait of Victorian
COLCHESTER

Photograph overleaf: North Hill, Colchester — AC

MKIN
se Furnisher
Valuer.
CONTRACTOR

A Portrait of Victorian COLCHESTER

PETER SHERRY

EPL

EGON PUBLISHERS LTD
Meeting House Lane, Church Street,
Baldock, Herts. SG7 5BP

First Published in 1982
by Egon Publishers, Ltd.
Meeting House Lane, Church Street, Baldock, Herts.

ISBN 0 905858 19 0

Printed in England by
S. G. Street & Co. Ltd
Meeting House Lane, Church Street,
Baldock, Herts. SG7 5BP

Contents

FOREWORD

For some time I have been interested in the Victorian period, and as a Colcestrian, I have concentrated my research on Victorian Colchester.

I began research for this book in 1963, and would like to dedicate it to all lovers of the old town.

Colchester is seeing many changes, and it is hoped that my book may be a record of a past era, and one that will be of interest to Colcestrians and visitors of all ages.

'A Portrait of Victorian Colchester' is for the general reader, and deals with such facets as markets and fairs, the coming of the railway, the three Town Halls, roads and streets, concerts, circuses and theatre, the military and the Salvation Army, cycles and cars, earthquake and weather, the Hythe, some political occasions, schools and children, the advent of popular photography, sport, the post, visits from famous people, patriotic occasions, churches, chapels and clocks, gaslight and electricity, Art and artists, the coming of industry, the early closing movement, the beginning of a museum and parks and a municipal library, public houses and beershops, the Temperance movement, the new sewage works and the new water tower (Jumbo).

I have made much use of contemporary newspapers and have quoted from them and woven characteristic Victorian phrases into the text.

PROLOGUE

When King William IV died in 1837, all Colchester shops except Obadiah White's, the baker's adjoining and those of the people called the Quakers were half closed. On that June Wednesday church bells were tolled for two hours, and, because of the King's funeral, Market Day was held on a Friday. All Saturday the shops were closed and bells were again tolled in the evening.

The proclamation of the young Queen, Victoria, was read out from the Moot Hall, Headgate and East Gate. Nearly two hundred assembled in the ballroom of the Three Cups Inn, when 'Long life to Her Majesty' was, 'drank with the most hearty cheers of the company'.

In the August of 1837, 'The Essex Standard' announced the publication of a 'spirited lithograph of the new Church of St. Botolph's and the ruins of the old church'. It had been executed from a drawing by Louisa, the wife of the Rev. James T. Round. Two months later the church was consecrated by the Bishop and the children of the Church of England School sang the 39th Psalm.

A Roman Catholic church was built in Priory Street in the same year.

December brought complaints about mud and filth that covered the pavement and carriageway of the High Street after the Saturday market. This remained untouched on Sunday, and on Monday was partly swept up in heaps in the centre of the street. 'The Essex Standard' was not very sympathetic. Ladies and gentlemen were informed that if they did not like the mud they should stay at home. Moreover, 'middling sort of folks and tag-rag and bobtailery in general' were told to leave the mud alone and not 'carry quantities upon their skirts and trousers'.

On Coronation Day 1838, thirty gentlemen saluted the Mayor on St. John's Green. Unfortunately, a blunderbuss accidentally injured one.

Streets were planted with large boughs and trees, and bells rang all day. Despite rain, the younger members of the family enjoyed sports in the castle bailey. As a result of charity, poor families were given plenty of meat and sixpence a head to regale themselves in their own houses. There were public dinners. At five o'clock men and boys uprooted the trees and dragged them to various spots to build bonfires. By nine o'clock there were ten large bonfires burning. The new era was also heralded by a great number of fireworks.

Entertainment was varied in the late eighteen thirties. Respectable folk enjoyed a Gala Day in the Botanic Garden when a military band played, quadrilles were danced and the flight of several fire balloons could be observed.

Respectable folk enjoyed too a bazaar in aid of the Colchester and Essex Hospital. There were four thousand visitors when elegant articles were exhibited on the stalls of lady shopkeepers.

Concerts at the Cups Hotel were also popular. Monsieur Thalberg, an unusual pianist, performed on an Erard new patent grand pianoforte brought expressly from London. Mr. Parry, Jun., the celebrated bass, sang several admired English and Italian airs, and two Swiss madamoiselles, Cecile and Albertine de Vanuz brought rustic charm, being accompanied on the pianoforte and flute.

Less 'respectable' folk visited the Theatre Royal, Queen Street to witness such shows as 'Macbeth', 'The Merchant of Venice', 'The Red Barn', 'The Country Squire', 'Her Husband's Ghost', 'The Castle Spectre', 'Miseralt' and 'Black Eye'd Susan'.

However, life in Colchester had its darker side with illness and crime. A ragged and dirty looking lad of sixteen was committed to fourteen days in the Borough Gaol for being drunk at the Duncan's Head in the parish of St. Mary's-at-the Walls. He had attempted to excite pity by feigning to be in strong fits.

Two policemen were assaulted by four men when they tried to quell a riot in Magdalen Street. Theft included a coal carter stealing from a coal merchant.

Infant schools such as the Hythe Infant School, were considered beneficial to the 'labouring classes'.

This opinion is indicated in these words:
'Keep children from the street — and the temptations to which they are exposed by the glaring gratifications in the shops and markets, until they are able to judge right from wrong'.

No doubt also with the 'labouring classes' in mind, a Sunday School was established in 1839 in the populous parish of St. Botolph.

There was great excitement for the children in November 1839 . . . Wombwells Menagerie. The monster elephant mounted on six iron-banded rollers, and drawn by twelve horses was seen passing North Bridge which trembled beneath its weight. The menagerie established itself immediately before the Moot Hall where it was brilliantly lighted by gas at night. The town was enlivened by the menagerie's excellent band.

THE FORTIES

Colcestrian Victorians were loyal in their attitude to Royalty. In February, 1840, the bells of several churches rang many peals to celebrate the Queen's marriage. A band paraded the streets proceeded by an elegant crown borne on a rich cushion and decorated with wedding favours and streamers of white ribbons. At dinner parties held at several inns, the royal couple were toasted enthusiastically. Business was generally suspended.

Two years later to celebrate the christening of the Prince of Wales, about two thousand schoolchildren were, 'regaled with plum cake and wine', coals were distributed the previous day, and five hundred pounds was the target to be raised in aid of the Colchester-Lying-in Charity.

In August, 1847, the 26th anniversary of Prince Albert's birthday was indicated by a display of the Royal Standard on the Town Hall.

In the forties Colchester still had, 'extensive prospects over the country in various directions'. Many people had little chance for exercise beyond a healthy field walk. In 1839 the ladies were disappointed to learn that the field walk at Lexden, once crossed by a decayed flap gate, was replaced by a rough stile.

The town was well supplied by pure, wholesome water. By an Act of Parliament a company had been established, the works being at the base of Balkerne Hill where there were excellent springs.

Colchester had twenty main streets, many smaller ones, and a great number of lanes and alleys, called walks, and rows of houses.

The footpaths and roads were laid with cobbles, which in time gave way to water-bound macadam. In May, 1840, there was an application for Head Street to be macadamised, because so much discomfort was caused day and night by passing vehicles. In the same year, the Mayor received complaints about the footpaths being dangerous, not having been sufficiently clear of snow. In 1847 the Commissioners issued an order that there would be a penalty if occupiers did not sweep the footways, or front of their houses and buildings, before eight every morning, except Sunday.

In 1844 there were plans to macadamise the High Street. Cabs and omnibuses continually passing caused an almost intolerable noise. Public business at the Town Hall was frequently greatly hindered by these vehicles clattering and jumping over the rough pebbles. Trade suffered, too, because, unless obliged, neighbours avoided the town to prevent damage to their horses and carriages.

The High Street had another danger. The persons whose job was to fix the sheep-pens for the market had the habit of laying hurdles along the carriageway on the Friday night.

In the same year there was a plan to remove St. Runwald's Church, the little church in the middle of High Street, and replace a new church on its site.

Before 1841 there had been town development on almost all the southern side of the town. From 1840 the town expanded 'irregularly' but continuously. The population in 1841 was 17,790, and in the nineteenth century St. Botolph's was the most heavily populated parish.

From 1819-1840 Colchester had witnessed the erection of a hospital, a church, a Provident Asylum for 'decayed tradesmen', a Corn Exchange, and other buildings of less importance. In 1840 the old Town Hall was described as, 'inconvenient, ugly, patched, tumbledown, miserable accommodation, held up by houses either side. Now it was the Town Gaol. Once it was the town theatre.' A Hall, Assembly Room, Courts, and offices, Public Library, Museum, etc. were all needed.

In the July of the next year, seventy three designs for a new Town Hall were arranged and on display in Mr. Jenkin's Lecture Room, St. John's Street.

By September, 1843, the Mayor, Dr. Roger Nunn, laid the first stone of this much needed municipal building. Less than a year later, R. Sanderson, M.P., inspected the building and, 'expressed himself much pleased with the appearance of the work'. Soon the shell was rapidly approaching completion; 'the court had been covered for several weeks . . . preparations made for fixing the roof of the principal portion of the structure including the public room, the magistrates room, and the council chamber'. It was opened in April, 1845. By January three years later, the Sessions Court was warmed by hot water.

The position of Colchester made it a natural agricultural centre. Meat, butter, poultry, vegetables and fruit were sold at the market place near the Town Hall. The corn market was near St. Peter's Church. The town supported the existing protection on foreign corn.

In May, 1842, there was a disastrous fire that at one time threatened to destroy much of High Street. St. Peter's vicarage was one residence to suffer. A much discussed

An interior of the 1844 Town Hall. Martin states, 'Thrift as much as conservatism probably dictated the plain, classical style of the new Town Hall. It was a four-square building. Although it included an assembly room, it was not lavishly planned, and its commodiousness, and therefore its dignity, was in question before the century was done' — CM.

John Vine's picture of the fire in High Street in 1842. This fire destroyed the Georgian vicarage of St. Peter's Church, and the site was used for a new Corn Exchange — EL.

project was to enlarge the Corn Exchange, and making an exterior stock market on part of the site, and in the rear of the recently consumed houses. The Corn Exchange was built in 1843.

The cattle market was held in the High Street. The corn and cattle market was on Saturday and the poultry and fruit market was on Wednesday. The market place was frequented by salesmen and purchasers every day.

In 1842, the inhabitants of Colchester became increasingly interested in the railway, and a year later on March 29th, the Eastern Counties Railway officially opened at Colchester. A party of ladies and gentlemen from London had already visited the town by railway and inspected the castle ruins, St. Botolph's Priory, and St. John's Abbey gate. The small wooden-shuttered railway station was built in the same year. This was a terminus. The railway was extended to Ipswich in 1846. Plans were soon in hand for a Railway Hotel with a lofty smoking tower, a fine prospect along the Colne Valley, and the adjoining ground (about an acre and a half) to be laid as an ornamental garden. By September this fine example of Italian architecture was completed.

In 1845 consternation arose amongst allotment tenants on Balkerne Hill and Harwich Road because it was suggested

John Vine's picture of the ruins in High Street after the fire, May 1st, 1842 — EL.

that a portion of each little plot would be needed for the proposed Colchester and Junction Railway.

In the same year the Railway Hotel, that had cost £15,000, closed after a brief, spirited, but unsuccessful campaign. By April, 1849, under the charitable auspices of S. M. Peto, Esq., M.P. for Norwich, it became an Asylum for infant idiots.

The coming of the railway once and for all emphasized the end of the Golden Age of coaching, although in 1846 Samson's Star Coach for Ipswich still left the George at nine o'clock in the morning. Two years previously, arrangements had been made for steam carriages on the road from Colchester, through Ipswich to Norwich.

Three fairs were held during each year.

A Midsummer Fair was held on July 5th on St. John's Green. In 1846 many horses were on display, but most of them were of an inferior description, and trade transacted was between dealers themselves. However, a few superior cart horses and colts were bought at high prices. As it was a market day the cattle and sheep fair was merged in the High Street market.

Just over two years previously there was trouble on one April Saturday in the High Street, materialising in a hostile collision between police and several of the 'horse-dealing fraternity'. The latter showed their discontent over a recent order by which it was prohibited to run and show horses, and only allowed this in a certain part of Head Street.

The St. Dennis Fair was held on October 30th and three following days. In the eighteen forties it was moved from Queen Street and High Street to the bottom of East Hill.

The third fair, the New Fair, was held on a field on the Harwich road on July 12th.

Except for shipping concerns, the town's trade was mainly the supply of the neighbourhood with manufactures in return for agricultural productions.

A silk manufacture was introduced in Colchester in about 1845. One factory was erected near the castle. Another was a large building, formerly the Barrack Tavern.

The town had many wind corn mills and several water mills. In 1840, the valuable watermill, East Mill, was purchased by E. Marriage of Chelmsford.

Malting was another important business.

The barracks had been pulled down after the Napoleonic War. All that remained were a few officers' houses, and these had become private dwellings. The breaking up of the barracks had for some time seriously affected the town. The military for years had helped to support the tradesmen and the 'labouring inhabitants'. Although the staff of the Essex Militia were still stationed here, the regiment had not been embodied for some years.

In 1843 the Paving Commissioners ordered that a portion of North Hill, opposite St. Peter's Church, should be taken off to the depth of about sixteen inches. The materials so obtained were placed in the hollow opposite the Marquis of Granby Inn. The thoroughfare was closed to vehicles for a short time to aid macadamizing. In the same year a new iron bridge, North Bridge, was erected. For a time there was a substantial temporary bridge for carriages and other traffic on payment of a small toll.

In this decade, Balkerne Hill was considered the most expensive to repair compared to any other road of similar length. It became almost impassable in the winter. Not only were there the natural disadvantages of the narrow descent, but the road was gullied in several places by open drains that had been badly made for some recently built cottages.

The worst place for drainage was the first hundred yards of Middleborough. Inhabitants had the unpleasant habit of throwing the drainage of their houses into the roads.

When there was heavy rain, the meadows and low grounds of the north were always in danger of much flooding.

In January, 1841, there was a heavy thunder and hail storm. After several hours of a strong wind, a sharp frost came, and a heavy snowfall covered the streets. Later in the month the ice and snow thawed rapidly, and the river Colne overflowed its banks. About thirty men were engaged in breaking the ice. At Middle Mill there were large quantities of ice. At East Bridge the water extended over the bridge and it could only be crossed by horses and carts. The Colne again overflowed four years later.

In 1845 it was found desirable to suppress Sunday trading. The solution was thought to be paying workmen on Friday or some other day except Saturday. It was a too common practice to buy food and other necessaries on a Sunday morning. There was an annoyance in Crouch Street coming from three shops selling cigars, etc. to young men and boys.

Another disturbance in the forties was the keeping of disorderly houses. Prostitutes could be seen passing through all the town streets, St. Leonard's parish was especially bad.

Despite the collapse of Hythe Bridge on April 1st, 1839, the Hythe, the port of Colchester, was a hive of industry. In 1840, the Rising Sun public house, a bonding yard, bonding vaults, malting, shipyard, dry dock, lime kiln, granaries, cottages, etc., were purchased by William Hawkins.

No fewer than twenty-seven coal merchants had yards on the waterfront or nearby. Also there were nine corn merchants and three lime burners. The famous Colchester boat-builder, Philip Sainty, had a yard here.

In 1842 the Hythe was approved by Her Majesty's Customs as a warehousing port for tea, coffee, sugar, butter, cheese, and a variety of other dry goods.

In January, 1843, the 'Swiftsure' reached the Hythe. This was the first steam vessel to do so, except Mr. Haley's small experimental boat, which was constructed at the port.

Many people visited the 'Swiftsure' for it was a well known commercial vehicle. Weekly she performed two voyages from Colchester to Greenwich and back.

By 1847 the lock and gates at the Hythe were extremely decayed, and by Act of Parliament, the channel was deepened as far as Fingringhoe.

Colchester welcomed the Penny Post. The Day Mail was established in 1845. In January 1846, some sensation was caused by the non-arrival of the day mail train from London till nearly four o'clock, the usual time being a quarter to one. Fortunately, there was no need for alarm, the reason being an insufficiency of steam which obliged the train to stop at Marks Tey till the arrival of another train, by which it was propelled to Colchester.

In the same year there was an extension of post time until ten o'clock in the evening instead of nine o'clock, a progressive step towards every possible facility for postal communication.

For some years it had been a complaint that those applying for, or receiving payment of money orders at the post office, were obliged to wait in the street, exposed to any weather until attended by the clerks. This state was rectified in 1848 by part of the private entrance being allowed for shelter.

In the following year the hours for receiving letters at the Colchester Post Office were as follows:

Down post closes at 9 o'clock.
Ditto for late letters at 9.50.
Up post closes at 10 o'clock.
No letters received after 10 o'clock for the up post.

It was pointed out too, that it would assist postmen greatly, if persons would arrange to send their letters so that they should not pass through the P.O. or be delivered on Sundays.

Until 1885 Colchester had two Members of Parliament, usually Conservative.

In July, 1841, there was a triumphal Conservative procession. Horses and carriages arrived at the Cups Hotel and the procession passed through the principal streets to the enthusiastic cheers of the townsfolk. A host of Conservatives thronged every house and waved true blue favours.

At four o'clock the procession returned to the Cups Hotel ready to honour Richard Sanderson and Sir Henry Smyth, Bart. An hour later a hundred gentlemen entertained the members to dinner, the chair being taken by Charles Gray Round.

In contrast, two years later, Sir John Tyrell with a party of ladies and gentlemen visited the Union Workhouse. They minutely inspected the different apartments and gave a certificate in the visitor's book, 'expressive of their high approbation of the arrangements of the house in all its departments'.

The Soup Fund was another way of helping the less fortunate. In January, 1849, soup was distributed at the castle. 705 quarts were shared out to the thankful applicants who had received tickets from the subscribers. Each ticket entitled the bearer to a quart of rich soup and 8 ozs of bread for one penny. The Committee had arranged to distribute 800 quarts of soup four days in the week. In some parishes to ensure a proper division of the benefit, committees met to deliver the tickets.

In the same year a report by the visiting Justices revealed that the prison was in excellent order, and that the health of the prisoners was good. At that time there were ten convicted felons, seven misdemeanants, four vagrants, one for trial at the Assizes, and one for further examination.

From 1835-1870 only voluntary societies such as the National Society and the British and Foreign School Society, aided by the parents weekly contribution could give an education in the three 'R's' for the majority.

Colchester had its share of private schools for the training of young ladies and young gentlemen. Such were the Colchester Academy, 12 Crouch Street, and North Hill Academy.

There was also the Royal Grammar School which in the eighteen forties was still situated in Culver Street. On a Tuesday afternoon in February 1847, between four and five, o'clock, the family of the Rev. J. Dunningham, the head-master, were alarmed by the discovery of a fire in the upper part of the house. Several neighbours were quickly on the spot. Soon the fire brigade was at hand, and there was an ample water supply from the premises of Mr. Brown, of the Sea Horse Inn.

From 1842 the Essex and Suffolk Insurance Society had three fire engines in Colchester. Twenty men were paid a small annual retaining fee. They attended all fires in the town and the surrounding district until 1879.

It was in the eighteen forties that the beginnings of a museum took root. In about 1840, William Wire, a born archaelogist, was the leading influence in starting a museum in the Colchester Literary Institute, St. John's Street.

In 1845 it was suggested that accommodation might be found for such a project in the new Town Hall. However, it was some years before somewhere worthy of the historic town could be established.

In 1840, in the Cups Hotel Assembly Room, the élite and gentry were entertained by none other than Liszt, whose pianoforte playing was renowned for its 'high brilliancy and most finished execution'. He played his 'Grande Marche Hongroise' and 'Grand Gallop Chromatique'. He also played a fine duet with Mr. Mori. Other entertainment at the Cups Hotel during this decade included Thiodon's attractive exhibition and scenery; the celebrated Rock Band; esteemed artistes like Grisi, Mario, Lablache, Benedict, Parry, the Ethiopian Singers and the well known American Serenaders.

There was also the powerful bass singing of Mr. Facquharson Smith; the comic songs of Mr. Moody; the wizardry of Mr. Jacobs; Mr. H. Russell, the composer of many popular songs and the Soirée Musicale of the Colchester Philharmonic Society.

Circuses in the eighteen-forties were mainly equestrian. A typical one, that of Mr. Bridge, jun., gave an exciting programme at the Castle Bailey in 1840. 'The dress, front and side boxes were beautifully embellished with a variety of highly finished paintings of the Horse. All were richly ornamented in gold and embossed frames and showed equestrian and gymnastic scenes. Five huge chandeliers of large and brilliant gas jets descended in the interior, whilst the elegant exterior was lighted by a number of gas lamps'.

Attractions in this circus included a pair of 'tamed llama ass zebras', the smallest horse in the world, only twenty seven inches high, and a Chinese flag fête on ten caparisoned steeds.

Moreover, there was the History of Allessandra Massaroni (the Brigand Chief), Rob Roy, Mazeppa, Master Selim Bridges on the tight rope, Mr. Walker on the corde volate, and Mr. Mackintosh's astonishing trampoline leaping, especially those over men standing on horses, through hoops on fire, and also over eight horses placed side by side. Finally, there was a magnificent Carnival Pageant.

In 1848 Colcestrians enjoyed a balloon ascent from the Botanic Garden by Mr. Green, the veteran aeronaut. 'The voyager waved farewell to his Colchester friends as the immense machine soared upwards. He was greeted by several rounds of cheers'.

In 1845, Mr. D. T. Davenport, a well known actor, secured the lease of the Theatre Royal. His daughter, Jean, was the 'star' of many productions.

On July 14th, and 15th, of this year, Macready appeared as 'Hamlet' and 'Richard II'.

Mr. Davenport's Benefit was on December 15th, 1848, and the production was 'Green Bushes, or One Hundred Years Ago'.

Histrionic fare in the eighteen forties was varied by tragedies, dramas, melodramas, comedies, farces, comic operas, burlesques, burletta and extravaganzas.

Only one church was built in Colchester in the 1840's. This was at Shrub End, an isolated hamlet, in 1845.

EL and National Monuments Record.
High Street 1854. Note the wide High Street looking east. To the left is R. Halls Fishmonger and Oyster Catcher and next to it is the Suffolk and Essex Insurance office. There are a few people on the pavement to the right including some looking at a hatter's window. It is a peaceful scene drawn by Josiah Parish.

THE FIFTIES

1851 was the year of the Great Exhibition, and it is no great surprise that patriotic Colchester sent a contribution. This materialised in Mr. Henry Aggio's highly elegant pianoforte of his own construction and design. 'Mrs. Aggio skilfully filled the upper part (which was divided into three compartments) with needlework on white satin. All the external woodwork, both plain and carved, was of gilt. This was relieved below and at the ends by silvered plate glass, and pedals of ivory. The keyboard made of the best ivory and ebony, added to the beautiful effect, and the construction of the instrument took nearly seven months'.

Another enterprising townsman was a certain Mr. Sallows who, in 1856, invented a most compact garden stool or form for horticultural and other fêtes.

Accidents in Victorian days often involved horses and horse-driven vehicles.

One Wednesday evening in November, 1850, as the omnibus from the Red Lion Hotel was proceeding up North Hill on its return journey from the 8.05 train, it collided with a pony and cart that had stopped at the top of the hill and completely overturned the vehicle. The frightened pony was in the act of starting off, but was prevented by the omnibus conductor. The cart owner and spectators were surprised to see the cart righted without any injury.

Six years later, in August, the pony phaeton of Charles Gray Round had just left Mrs. Round at St. Mary's Terrace when, as the groom was driving the pony from the terrace, for some unknown reason, the animal took fright. It started swiftly along Lexden Road, through Head Street and High Street. The phaeton came into contact with a water cart near the Goat and Boot public house, East Hill. The groom was thrown out but was uninjured.

One June Saturday in 1857, Ensigns Pritchard and Cox of the 13th depot, accompanied by a servant, were proceeding to the railway station in a dog cart drawn by a spirited horse. The latter was frightened by a train which was passing the bridge and this caused the vehicle to be upset. The dog cart was dashed to pieces. The occupants were severely bruised, but Ensign Pritchard was able to proceed by train to London.

Another accident occurred in January, 1858, on a Saturday afternoon at about five o'clock. Cab driver, Henry Boyden, had just left the Fleece Inn, Head Street, to convey a gentleman to the train, when a horse ran against a wheelbarrow filled with manure, which had been left in the street. The barrow was broken to pieces and the knees of the horse were severely cut. The carriage of J. W. Green Esq., containing only the driver, was turning the corner from High Street and a collision was only just avoided.

In July, 1851, the newly built British National School in Magdalen Street, was opened on a Monday morning. The building was considered, 'quite an ornament in that part of town'. It was designed by Mr. Hayward and built in the Gothic style of red brick with stone dressings.

In the following year there was a favourable report on North Hill Infant School. 'The children proved, both by their quietness and order and the way in which they acquitted themselves, that their new school-mistress, Miss Manning, had taken great pains in their management and instruction'.

Children had a chance to enjoy themselves. In August, 1852, the juveniles of St. Giles Day and Sunday School had their treat. This was held in the meadow opposite the Rector's residence on the Mersea road after first assembling at the church. After being amused with swings, racing, football, jumping and other sports, they were 'summoned to partake of a bountiful supply of tea and bread and butter'. Before the children eventually dispersed each was given a parting gift of fruit and buns.

It was in the same year that the Grammar School moved from Culver Street to its new premises in Lexden Road. Two years later the 'Essex Standard' informs its readers that the 'pupils of the upper class have adopted the full academical costume of cap and gown'.

There was a complaint in 1855 from those who ran the Ragged School in Osborne Street, that the low theatricals and the noisy crowds could have a harmful influence upon its pupils.

In July, two years later, about 150 children, girls and boys from the Ragged School, were entertained at a rural

Master's house and schoolroom of Colchester Royal Grammar School, Lexden Road, that was built in 1852 by Henry Hayward — AC.

fête in the pleasant grounds of W. Stannard, Esq., of Distillery Mill. This surely had a most beneficial influence. The children had sports in two paddocks and an abundant supply of tea, bread and butter and plum cake. After tea there were more sports until about eight in the evening. Then in groups of two or three circles the children sang pleasantly in front of the lawn. Before dispersing they were given buns, lemonade and strawberries.

In June, 1859, Mr. Charles Gray Round, declined selling the garden grounds and stables on the south side of the castle as a site for the New National Schools.

However, the same gentleman did assist in the development of a museum project. In 1852, Alderman Henry Vint bequested his valuable collection of bronzes to the town. Some of these had been found in Colchester. Three years later, Mr. Round, as treasurer of the newly established Archaelogical Society, and owner of the castle, allowed the chapel crypt to be used as a public museum by the Corporation and Archaelogical Society.

In 1850, Mr. Joseph Clarance, a world wide celebrity took over the lease of the Theatre Royal. One November night in that year, Louisa Foote Hay, 'the Liverpool Lind', a delightful vocalist, sang beautiful melodies and Mr. Dace accompanied at the pianoforte.

Almost three years later appeared Mr. Robert Houdin, the French conjurer. 'Among his leading tricks, the spontaneous supply of hot punch dispensed, ad lib, among the clamorous occupants of the pit; the production from an ordinary looking drawing-portfolio of culinary utensils, bird cages, and other bulky articles and plentifully yield of bouquets, bonbons, fans, newspapers, etc., from his magic cornucopia were naturally the most popular, from the spirited scramble to which their distribution gave rise'.

In 1856 Charles Gill became lessee and manager of the theatre. In January of that year audiences were charmed by M. Desaris' exhibition of trained dogs and monkeys, and three months later officers of the Essex Rifles (Militia) staged 'A Grand Amateur Night' for the benefit of the Colchester Hospital.

In 1851, the once attractive Botanic Garden became a scene of desolation. The shrubs had been bought and the land given to the Land Society for building allotments.

At the Cups Hotel the Distin family entertained. The staple of the evening was saxhorn performances, but these were contrasted by the 'vocal efforts of Miss M. O. Connor and a pianoforte solo by Mr. Norman'.

The Collins family also entertained there, the chief items being several solos on the violin and concertina. Miss Emma Collins presided at the pianoforte, whilst Miss Victoria skilfully handled the violincello.

The Cups Hotel was also the scene of Miss Fanny Vining reading Shakespeare's 'Much Ado about Nothing' and in 1858 the Sisters Sophia gave their 'Sketches From Nature'.

In 1852, Mr. Ellis Roberts, harpist to His Royal Highness, The Prince of Wales, assisted by Miss Blanche Young, of the Royal Academy and Royal Polytechnic, London, gave a Morning and Evening Entertainment at the Colchester Literary Institution. In the morning members paid a shilling for admission, and non-members two shillings. In the evening members paid nothing, and non-members one shilling each.

At the Public Hall, in 1853, Mr. Henry Phillips gave an admirable illustrated lecture on the sacred songs of Handel and Haydn. At the Town Hall, three years later, Colcestrians enjoyed the 'mirth provoking art' of Mr. Woodins Olio of Oddities, with his, 'wonderful pieces of comic portraiture'. Also at the Town Hall, in 1852, Mrs. Fanny Kemble read the first part of Shakespeare's, 'Henry IV'.

Also in the fifties, Mr. and Mrs. German Reed entertained. Mrs. Reed impersonated various characters and sang several English, French and Italian songs. A crowded audience enjoyed a concert by vocal artistes from the Drury Lane Opera, the main attraction being Mademoiselle Piccolomi.

In September, 1855, photography came to Colchester in the form of Mr. Beattie's picture rooms . . . 'a truly unique travelling establishment was located temporarily at the castle bailey. On exhibition were some fine portraits of Colchester worthies. By this time it was possible for anyone to have a, 'faithful likeness of those whose image and memory were desired to perpetuate'.

In August, 1859, the Colchester Archery Fête was held at the beautiful ground of P. O. Papillon, Esq., M.P. The Archery Club had been established in the previous summer. The ladies especially proved 'skilful adepts in target practice'. The archers had dinner in a marquee in a picturesque yew grove and all concluded with a merry dance. The marquee was illuminated with variegated lamps.

Also in this year the Colchester Public Baths were opened again in Osborne Street. A water supply came direct from the Water Works so the water was purer. There was a large first class swimming bath, with dressing boxes, etc., a second class swimming bath, and three first class private hot, cold, or shower baths. When necessary all were lighted by gas.

The High Street was infested with pickpockets on Market days. Many beer shops and public houses were not only the scene of drunkenness, but of 'gambling, marts of prostitution, and the most abhorrent licentiousness'. In May, 1854, because of the additional malt tax, the brewers and publicans increased the charge for porter by a half penny and penny per pot.

Certain customs were kept alive in this decade.

On January 1st, 1854, the ancient New Year's bequest of presenting a penny roll to every unmarried person resident in the parish of St. Leonard's was carried out. Several hundred of both sexes benefited.

For St. Valentine's Day of the same year nearly three thousand letters were posted. 'The difficulty of reading some of the addresses did not help the postmen in their unenviable job of assisting the lovelorn'.

On November 5th, 1853, the children were disappointed to learn that, 'as it was a Market Day, the Mayor issued a warning against the making of fireworks in the public streets'.

In 1853, an alteration was carried out in the Church of St. Mary's when the large west window was restored after having been bricked up for many years. Also a very fine arch, previously hidden, could be seen by removing the lath and plaster partition at the back of the gallery and placing the organ in the tower. This also gave space for fifty more seats.

Good Friday was observed with reverence in 1854 when all tradesmen, except three or four Quakers, closed their businesses. Large congregations filled churches and chapels.

St. Giles must have had one of the youngest church organists ever, when Master Arthur Winterbon, from a well known musical family, was appointed. He was only eleven years old.

North Station photographed between 1854 and 1865 – CM.

In June, 1855, All Saints Church was closed so that it could be repewed and repaired. Divine Service was held in the chapel at the castle until the alterations were finished.

Four years later St. Peter's Church was restored.

It is also interesting to note that it was whilst sheltering from a winter storm in 1850 in a Primitive Methodist chapel founded in Artillery Street in 1839, that Charles Haddon Spurgeon heard the sermon that transformed him into a leading evangelist of the Age.

In 1854, the Colchester railway station was enlarged. In February of the same year, because of the alteration in train times, the bags for the up morning mail had to be despatched from the Colchester post office at ten o'clock. The box for the up letters for the day mail was closed at a quarter to ten, but later this was extended five minutes.

A year later, the news of the fall of Sebastopol was received by telegraph. The bells of St. Peter's Church were immediately rung until nearly midnight.

In November, 1855, the letter box at the Colchester office was open until nine in the morning for letters by the up mail. In the following year pillar boxes were placed in Crouch Street, St. Botolph's Street and Northgate Street. Collections were made at nine o'clock in the morning and at eight o'clock in the evening.

Because of changes in the mail train in May of the following year, letters for the morning mail had to be posted at the principal office by nine o'clock.

In January, 1858, a new arrangement extended the day mail via the Eastern Counties and Eastern Union lines to Norwich and Yarmouth. The London bags for this train were received at eleven o'clock and delivered within an hour.

A Directory for 1855 states that in Colchester there were 'many merchants and shipowners, a customs house, an inland revenue office, banks, a savings bank, marine and fire assurance companies, breweries, vinegar works, newspaper offices, iron and brass foundries, tanneries, rope and sail works, machine works, coach works, lime, whiting and tobacco pipe factories'.

The East Hill Brewery was well known for its celebrated light bitter beer which was considered a 'most wholesome and nourishing beverage' and had a large sale in Colchester and surrounding district.

There was a distillery at Culver Street that had a bottled port cellar nearly a hundred feet long.

Throughout the Victorian era, High Street developed. One new shop in 1857 was that of George Rickword, upholsterer, cabinet maker, undertaker, and auctioneer who was established eight years earlier. The new building contained for sale, 'a collection of useful and beautiful furniture and at the same time having plenty to make cottages comfortable, even luxurious, at a reasonable price'.

There was an Early Closing Movement as early as 1855. The principal drapers had agreed to close their premises at seven o'clock in the evening in the winter. By November of that year book sellers also wished to follow this example.

In April, 1858, the Colchester Penny Bank, or Savings Bank, was started for sums varying from one penny to three shillings. It was opened every Monday evening at the Town Hall. At every meeting night there were names of several new depositors.

A stereoscopic view of the market in the High Street. At one time the market was moved to Lord's Land west of Balkerne Hill, but it returned to the High Street — CM.

In 1855, there were plans to remove the cattle market from the High Street. Some feared that this would result in the High Street being deserted. It would 'then indeed not be a typical market day with its filth, shouting, and the beating of animals, and the roaring of the larger and beating or squeaking of the lesser animals'.

Two years later, it was obvious that there was insufficient room in the High Street for the cattle market. There was concern for the safety of people, especially in the narrow part of Head Street. Neat stock, horses, and colts particularly, needed more space although the sheep and pig market could still be kept in hurdles. 'A farmer was lifted from the ground by an infuriated cow chasing a dog, a worthy miller was knocked down, and there were several minor accidents'.

In September, 1858, an animal lover wrote to the 'Essex Standard', protesting against the cruel treatment of cattle and sheep. It advised the removal of cattle altogether from the streets or to 'place policemen to arrest the men and boys who could be seen from the Cups Hotel every market day so fearfully striking the cattle on their horns and head with their full strength with bludgeons more suitable for hedge-stakes'.

There was no doubt by the middle of this decade that Colchester was again to be a garrison town. By July, 1855, considerable progress had been made in the foundation of the wooden huts, etc. that were to be the new encampment. There were to be twenty-five wells, which, from a very few inches beneath the soil, passed to a considerable depth through red sand.

The camp was laid out between the Old Heath and Mersea roads, and was later to be extended over the Abbey Field.

Later in 1855, some of the buildings were roofed in, and were progressing with interior fittings. In fact the operation proved a very busy scene, and by September there were huts to accommodate nineteen battalions.

In contrast, in the same month, the band of the Essex Rifles performed in public, every Tuesday and Thursday afternoon in the Avenue, Lexden Road. In 1856 the garrison chapel was opened.

In April, 1856, Prince Albert visited the new camp in which he showed great interest. He found an enthusiastic crowd giving a loyal demonstration. About a thousand flags flew on North Hill, Head Street, High Street, Queen Street, St. Botolph's Street, the Military Road and East Hill.

In July of the same year, the Foreign Legion camp became the scene of public Sunday performances by a military band; something that was frowned upon by some Victorians.

Less than a year later, the Duke of Cambridge passed down East Hill and entered the camp by the east gate near the Camp Church, 'where he was received by Sir William O'Mallery, barrackmaster, and where the troops had been drawn up in continuous columns, right in front, to receive him'.

There was another important town development in 1856. On a beautiful April day, the cemetery was consecrated by the Rt. Rev., Bishop of Rochester. The buildings consisted of an entrance house, two chapels and a receptacle house.

Less than a year later the scheme to remove Middle Row, in the High Street, began. A small shop that adjoined the east end of St. Runwald's Church, was demolished.

It is interesting to note that the High Street in March, 1856, was not watered although principal streets such as St. Botolph's Street, East Hill, Head Street, etc., were. In the same month, Crouch Street and Lexden Road, as far as St. Mary's Terrace, was smothered with dust for three days.

Three years later a well that had recently been dug near the top of Hythe Hill provided a water supply.

In 1854, six thousand pounds had been spent on obtaining another two feet of water at the Hythe. This enabled larger ships to berth. Colchester exported mainly corn, malt and flour. Cargoes, chiefly from colliers, came in lighters from Wivenhoe. Foreign trade was small, consisting mainly of Spanish wine, Dutch oilcake and Baltic timber. In the 1850s the river had some shipbuilding and there was much coastal traffic.

One January night in 1853 there was a gale of some violence. A chimney was blown off at the Hythe. A large piece of lead was stripped from the house and carried some distance by the wind. On the opposite side of the street a ridge tile was carried through a window. The roof of All Saints Church was stripped of some tiling and in St. Mary's churchyard some large branches were torn from the trees.

It is strange to observe that in the same January, sprigs of may could be seen in bud in Mr. W. Bunting's garden on North Hill, and that a butterfly flew over a garden bed in St. Mary's Terrace.

Six years later, thunderstorms in June brought several casualties in Magdalen Street. 'A chimney of the Duke of York public house was shattered, some water troughing melted and several panes of glass were broken. A horse in an adjoining stable was knocked down and stupefied, and a milkman and a lady he was serving were both knocked down by the electric fluid'.

Photograph overleaf:
High Street circa 1860. Looking west. Note to the left Colchester Bazaar and bookseller and stationer. To the right is part of St. Runwald's Church and the exterior of the 1844 Town Hall can be seen. There are only a few pedestrians and a few horse drawn vehicles — EL.

COLCHESTER BAZAAR
BOOKSELLER
34 PARSONS
PARSONS 34
33 RUST 33

The Sixties

In May, 1860, the bells of St. Peter's Church rang throughout the day to celebrate the Queen's birthday. The Town Hall and churches also hoisted flags to honour the occasion.

At the end of the following year, in common with the rest of Britain, Colchester mourned the death of the Prince Consort. On a cold December Sunday, the Royal Standard flew half mast high from the Town Hall, and between two and three o'clock all the church bells were tolled.

For some months in 1863 the town had been subject to epidemics of smallpox, scarlet fever and measles. Three years later a case of cholera caused some anxiety, and in May 1867 there were three cases of smallpox.

The first public fountain was erected in Colchester in 1860. It was designed by Charles Foster Hayward and stood at the corner of St. Nicholas churchyard, next to the High Street.

In February of the following year the need for a Public Garden was expressed; 'somewhere where a band could play; somewhere that was safer than the Lexden Road, which was almost the only promenade, and that was busy with horses, carriages or cattle'.

St. John the Baptist's Church was built in 1862 on the Ipswich road.

In July, 1863, the church clock projecting from St. Peter's Church was finished and started its 'time-recording duties' on a Wednesday evening. The hours were struck on a large tenor bell in the tower, and the quarter chimes on the smaller bells. In the following year the clock was wantonly damaged by a stone being thrown at the face, but it was easily repaired.

The town had its bell ringers and on one Monday evening in February, 1866, in commemoration of ringing one thousand changes on St. Peter's Church bells, they sat down to a good supper at Mr. Frederick Hyam's Stockwell Arms, in Stockwell Street.

St. Peter's Church was closed for three weeks in August of the following year, so that cleansing and repairing operations could be carried out. During this time services were taken at the Town Hall.

St. Paul's Church was built in North Station Road in 1867.

It was in this decade, too, that the Rev. C. H. Spurgeon preached two sermons at the Baptist Chapel, Eld Lane. The two collections went towards expenses for the new schoolroom.

At the Market, in March, 1860, posts and ropes were used to keep the neat stock within prescribed limits on the north side of High Street. However, from the distance between the posts the intended barrier yielded so readily to the pressure of the cattle, that the experiment was not considered successful.

Two years later, in October, the stock market was held for the last time in High Street. The new cattle market was to be on the site of the old tan yard premises in Middleborough, between the foot of North Hill and North Bridge. Soon the market place was opened. Crowds of cattle no longer blocked the High Street, 'making the air vocal with their cries and redolent of their odour'.

The drinking public fountain was opened in the new cattle market in August 1865. It was the gift of T. J. Miller, Esq., M.P., and was made chiefly of Portland stone and white brick. The base was of Haytor granite and the pilastes of polished Peterhead granite. 'The centre slab and basin are of Serpentine marble, prepaid by the South Metropolitan Drinking Fountain Company, with a shell of white porcelain from which the water flows. Below is a stone basin, 'intended as a drinking-place for dogs'. The overflow was to be used for cattle in the market itself. Two appropriate lamps surmounted the fountain. To complete its appearance, Messrs H. and J. Joslin supplied 'a very handsome bronze double gas lamp, each burner being enclosed in a globular glass frame'.

Two months later the Market had to be closed for a few weeks to beasts and sheep, to prevent the spread of cattle plague in the neighbourhood. This plague still lingered in August, 1866, in the parish of Lexden.

By the 1860s, the milling capacity at East Mill had developed so much that the channel from the Hythe to the mill needed deepening. This work was completed by 1865 and instead of loading and unloading at the Hythe, as was previously done, sailing barges were able to berth at the mill.

Penny Readings became fashionable in this decade. In Colchester these were held at the Public Hall, through the auspices of the Colchester Library and Reading Rooms. The readings were considered, 'altogether a success, and many of the pieces were read with admirable taste'.

The first Thames barges at East Mill, 1865 — CM.

In 1862, Mr. Coe of the Haymarket Theatre read selections from Shakespeare, Sheridan, Tennyson, Bulwer, etc. These were varied by vocal and instrumental music by such artistes as Madle, Georgi and Miss Blanche Percy.

In the same year the Colchester National Central Schools celebrated the fiftieth year of their formation. These schools were thought to be a 'wide-spread blessing to the industrial classes of this town and neighbourhood'.

A start was made on building a school house in Balkerne Lane in April 1864.

About a year later, schoolboys from the Union Home were treated by Major and Mrs. Harker, of West Terrace, Lexden Road. They were given plum cake, strawberries, cherries and other fruits. The boys gave three hearty cheers to show their gratitude. After playing some tunes on their fifes and drums, and singing several songs they 'departed much delighted with their entertainment'.

The new rooms of the Colchester Ragged Evening Schools were opened in Stanwell Street one week in January, 1866. There were eighty-five girl pupils and one hundred and thirty-eight boys.

The local press thought that November 5th had degenerated into 'the Guys, being chiefly small boys, bedizened with frills of coloured paper and their faces masked or blackened with soot'.

In the following October, boys bowling hoops on the pavement were liable to a fine of 40 shillings.

Also in 1867, Mrs. Bree's Industrial School for Girls started. The rules were as follows:

1. The hours of attendance to be from seven o'clock in the morning until six in the afternoon, from the 1st of April to the 1st of November and for the remainder of the year from eight o'clock to half-past four.
2. Any girl may bring her breakfast and eat it at school.
3. Dinner to be given at school.
4. Girls will be admitted between the ages of 12 and 16, and continue there six months, and if at the end of that time, their conduct be good they will be provided with a good place and a proper dress.
5. The girls will be taught cooking, needle and laundry work by experienced teachers.
6. Lastly, all girls will be required to attend on Sundays their usual places of worship, and Sunday schools.

A year later a school was proposed for the Hythe for, 'In no part of Colchester is such provision more urgently needed'.

In September, 1860, the castle crypt was used as a museum, and various townspeople gave donations and contributions. By 1866, more space was needed and the gallery leading to the crypt was also used. The first curator was Mr. Charles Hampton.

Because of the frost in January, 1861, the Eastern Counties Company announced that as a precaution against accidents on the railway, more time would be allowed 'to the fast and express trains'.

Four years later the Colchester station was rebuilt, and by 1867 the Tendring Hundred Railway had run a line to St. Botolph's. In fact, on an August Monday in 1866, there was a train accident when the Cambridge goods train left the Hythe Station just after one o'clock in the afternoon, when it got off the metals near East Street gates. Nothing more sensational resulted than blocking the lines for a few hours. The 1.50 train from St. Botolph's Station was not despatched.

Passengers were conveyed in cabs from that station to North Station to meet the up train.

Pickpockets were still a danger in Colchester. About half-past-eight one April Saturday in 1863, when Mr. Sowman was standing in a crowd near St. Nicholas Church, High Street, 'some adroit thief stole from his waistcoat pocket, his watch, with which he got safely away.' Two years later the 'pocket picking fraternity' continued to visit the town.

Other thieves, in May, 1869, robbed Mr. G. Guiver, landlord of the George Hotel, of a quantity of plate, principally spoons, valued at about thirty pounds.

Drink was one of the prevailing evils of Victorian days. In the 1860's, Colchester had an unnecessarily large number of public houses and beershops. These were considered to produce 'a most injurious influence upon the morals and happiness of the working classes'.

To counteract this evil in the town, such people as Mr. John Ripley, of Leicester, agent to the East of England Temperance League, gave an entertainment at the Temperance Hall, Osborne Street, in April, 1863. Before a crowded audience there were teetotal recitations and melodies, 'concluding with a deeply moving address on "Moral Cowards and Moral Heroes." '.

Money orders at the Colchester post office in 1861, were issued from nine o'clock in the morning until six o'clock in the evening. Letters could be registered up to within half-an-hour of the letter box closing for each mail. The post office closed for the sale of stamps and other business at ten o'clock at night.

In March, two years later, as a result of the arrival of the daily mails from Ipswich, Bury, Norwich, etc., there was a third letter delivery in the town starting at half-past-two o'clock.

A pillar letter-box that stood near the King's Arms public house, Crouch street, was moved in November, 1865, to opposite St. Mary's Terrace, Lexden Road. A wall letter-box was fixed at the Headgate end of Crouch Street, between Mr. Moore's and the Bull Inn.

The vacant space at the end of St. Runwald's Church, and the part in front of the Corn Exchanges, was authorised, in February, 1861, as cab stands in the High Street, by the Town Commissioners.

Another form of transport caused much annoyance in December, 1869. An increasing number of velocipedists pursued 'their erratic course along the thoroughfares of the town, to the no small danger of steady going pedestrians frequenting the pavement and footpath'.

Religious services were sometimes held at the Theatre Royal, in 1860.

On a November Friday evening in the following year, the Colchester public had the opportunity for the first time to hear the popular author, Charles Dickens, read from his own works. Not only was the theatre filled, but there was not room to satisfy all the applications for seats. On this occasion, Dickens read 'Nicholas Nickleby at Mr. Squeer's School', and the trial of 'Bardell v. Pickwick' from 'The Pickwick Papers'. 'Mr Dickens' style of reading, without the least apparent effort, brings his characters before the mind's eye with great force and raciness, backed of course with the powerful authority of the author's own rendering'.

Mr. and Mrs. George Case (the latter better known as Grace Egerton) gave a very varied and interesting entertainment, consisting of impersonations, anecdotes and songs etc., by Mrs. Case, and some superb performances on the violin and concertina by Mr. Case.

In May, 1865, came Burtons Original Christy Minstrels. 'The various pieces, both comic and pathetic, were all in excellent taste and harmony'.

Amateur theatricals were a craze in mid-Victorian times. In August, 1865, for the benefit of the County Asylum at Brentwood, a distinguished company, including Sir Thomas and Lady Barrett-Lennard of Belhus, Mr. Hozier of the Life Guards, and Captain Stacey, of the Scots Fusilier Guards, appeared in a comedietta, 'Delicate Ground', which was followed by the drama, 'A Sheep in Wolf's Clothing'.

About two years later, Harry Clifton, the popular vocalist, gave a concert at the theatre. Audiences were down, possibly owing to the election, but those who came enjoyed hearing some of the popular songs of the day sung by their author. Also appearing were Miss Fanny Edwards (contralto), Miss Annie Kinnaid (serio comic), and Mr. Frank Sadler (buffo).

The theatre, in 1867, was described as 'large and commodious' and as 'frequently occupied by various companies'. In June of that year, for one night, the officers of the

6th Inniskilling Dragoons, under the patronage of Col. Crawley, presented the farce of 'Little Toddlekins', with 'Macbeth Travestie'.

The local press announced in January, 1869, that 'the Colchester Theatre is now open for a short season, under the management of Mr. C. H. Stanley, late of the Adelphi and Olympic Theatres, with Miss Clara Griffiths as directress'.

Entertainment was also given at the Public Hall. In December, 1862, Mr. Charles Mathews, the celebrated dramatist, gave his entertainment, 'At Home', one Thursday evening.

In the following December, Gompertz's Panorama showed scenes of Italy and the Rhine.

For a week in May, six years later, Mr. Alfred Stodare presented his show 'consisting of marvellous tricks and illusions' to numerous audiences. 'With less than the usual paraphernalia of professors of the 'black art', Mr. Stodare cleverly and neatly performed a number of illusions, which, with the Indian basket trick, and the peculiar manifestations of the new-world-renowned 'Sphinx', were much appreciated'.

An opera troupe called 'Beal's Star Entertainment' came in the September of 1868. A correspondent to the 'Essex Standard' found two faults, namely; 'the too powerful singing of one of the female singers', and 'the shortness of the attire of the dancing girl'.

Messrs. Pavitt and Boulton entertained a year later, in May. 'Mr. Pavitt was especially good in his ventriloquism and caricature of a penny reading, and Mr. Boulton's impersonations of Mrs. Chillingstone, Mary, a village maiden, and Lady Jane Desmond were very lifelike and amusing'.

Mr. George Grossmith, the well known humorous entertainer gave 'Pickings from Pickwick' at the Town Hall in May, 1861, with the patronage of the Mayor, Colonel Street, W. W. Hawkins, Esq., Dr. Brice, and other dignitaries.

Seven years later, in January, a very select audience consisting mostly of ladies, enjoyed listening to a Welsh musician named Aptommas, the Paganini of the harp. He brilliantly played works by Beethoven, Mendelssohn, Handel, Alvara, and some fantasies introducing Irish, Scottish and Welsh melodies.

Sometimes Colcestrians provided their own amusement. A party of twelve amateur musicians, in August, 1860, volunteered their services for a brass band.

An entertainment was given at St. James' Sunday School-Rooms seven years later, on behalf of the Young Men's Mutual Improvement Society. A magic lantern was exhibited and several songs sung, and 'pieces of music performed by members of the society, the church choir, and others'.

The pupils of the Essex Hall Institution were given an excellent vocal and instrumental concert one Friday evening in January, 1860. This was performed by Mr. J. Sidney Jones and eight others. 'The room still had its decorations and one very beneficial effect of the delightful entertainment was that one little girl, who was unable to walk alone when she came to Essex Hall last July, went unaided right across the large dining hall, from the healthy stimulus of the music.'

The Literary Institution was the scene of another very agreeable music entertainment four years later.

Middleborough looking south up North Hill. Middleborough joins North Hill and North Station Road. It was anciently called Turpe Street and Middleburgh — AC.

Circuses were still very popular. The circus procession of Howes and Cushings Circus, in October, 1860, however, resulted in an accident. As it passed through Middleborough, at the bottom of North Hill, a pony belonging to Messrs. Lee and Baker took fright and knocked over 'an aged pieman John Johnson, with whose cry of "all hot", the streets of Colchester have so long been familiar.'

Seven years later, Messrs. Powell, Footit and Clarke's Circus included the 'unusual attraction of a performing hippopotamus'. In the same year, Edmond's (Late Wombwell's) Menagerie entered into the town with an 'extensive collection of animals'.

An accident occurred to a Mr. Henry Hayhoe in July, 1864. He assisted with one of the large swinging boats at St. John's Green fair. 'Trying to stop one, which was moving quickly, he was carried up on it. On going down again he was doubled underneath. Still holding onto it he was carried up again. As he let go he fell backwards to the ground.'

There was an entertainment for about three hundred children of soldiers belonging to the camp schools at the Camp in January, 1862. 'After tea, the delight of the juveniles reached the culminating point when the curtain drawn from before a stage at the bottom of the room disclosed a gigantic Christmas tree lighted with lamps and profusely hung with toys, sweetmeats, bonbons, fancy articles, etc. which the ladies kindly proceeded to distribute.'

In June of the following year, the band of the Essex Rifles Militia, played every Monday evening until the end of August, in the Avenue, Lexden Road, starting at half-past six o'clock.

In October, 1863, there was a hurricane at about half-past four one Friday afternoon. It caused considerable damage to unfinished buildings, scaffolding, etc. at the new Cavalry Barracks, damaging roofs of the Barrack Stores and Royal Engineers Department. A large walnut tree was blown down in the Pinnacle Gardens, and a large poplar tree 'was injured in Mr. Hawkin's timber yard, Magdalen Street'.

By 1864, the barracks was doubled and there was a Cavalry Camp inside Butt Road. Five years later, the War Office decided to enclose the Cavalry Barracks by a brick and iron palisading from the east side. The part near the road had been walled in from the beginning.

The German Legion Camp in 1868. The German Legion was also in Colchester during the Crimean War and they married many Colchester girls — CM.

Colcestrians enjoyed some sport in this decade. On an August Monday in 1863, nearly two thousand spectators watched a 'novel and exciting boat race' on North River. The competing boats were Mr. Harrington's, 'Lilley', and Mr. Cobbold's 'June'. The crew consisted of seven gentlemen from Colchester. The course was from North Bridge to Chopping's Mill and back.

The frost in January 1864, provided sport for skaters in various parts of the town, especially at the Distillery Pond, the Bourne Pond, the Moat Farm, Lexden, and North River.

Five years later, at Christmas, the skaters also took advantage of the frost, 'but it must be added, that, at several places, principally the Distillery Pond, the ice could not support the weight suddenly brought upon it, and collapsed, placing those who confined themselves to it, in considerable jeopardy'.

The Colchester Cricket Club, in January, 1865, obtained a lease of twenty one years, to use part of the old barrack ground, a large field facing Wimpole Lane, which was within easy access of the town centre.

The Colchester artist, John Vine (1808-1867). He was an artist in Colchester for 36 years. Although born in comparative poverty and without arms, with deformed fingers he could hold a pencil or brush. He wore a cloak or cape to hide his deformity. He was called Gentleman John Vine because he married a lady of good birth. He produced many paintings, chiefly in oils, but he was also successful in water colours — CM.

Benjamin Cant, a well known cultivator of Colchester roses — CM.

Two years later, on a May Thursday, many people gathered in Crouch Street and Lexden Road to watch a militia man, George Dawson, styled as 'The Essex Stag'. He had undertaken to run ten miles in one hour; a feat accomplished with apparent ease with thirteen minutes to spare.

The Early Closing Movement continued in the sixties Most shops, in June, 1866, were to be closed at five o'clock during the summer months. About fifty tradesmen from High Street agreed, and about forty in St. Botolph's Street and Wyre Street. However, at that time, the grocers did not give their support. In January of the following year, the chemists came to a unanimous agreement to close their shops at eight o'clock in the evening, except on Saturdays.

During 1868 this movement aimed at all shops closing at four o'clock in the afternoon on one day in the week. The majority of drapers and bootmakers resolved to close. At first the grocers remained open, but later they agreed to close at four. The ironmongers intended to close at seven. It is to be noted that in their leisure time, 'some of the young men had a very agreeable game of cricket at the Abbey Farm'.

The Local Board of Commissioners, in November, 1862, declined to pave and light the new streets that had been built on the old Botanic Garden, East Hill. The inhabitants of about forty, raised a subscription on one Monday evening. Eventually Roman Road and Castle Road were lighted with paraffin lamps placed on posts. About twenty of the owners celebrated the event with an excellent supper at 'The Roman Urn'.

Throughout the Victorian period the town centre was lit by gas. In September, 1867, the directors of the Colchester Gas Company announced a reduction in the price of gas, and a considerable reduction in the hire of meters.

Two Colchester artists came into the news in this decade. One Tuesday evening in February, 1866, Mr. Josiah Parish, an artist who lived in Head Street, when stepping out of his backdoor, heard a peculiar sound. He discovered that the crown of a well had given way and the well proved to be of some depth.

The other artist was armless, Gentleman John Vine, who lived in a cottage in Maldon Road and died in 1867. Despite his handicap he had a great reputation for his pictures of cattle, horses and dogs.

It is interesting to note that in April, 1867, Mr. Holman Hunt's celebrated picture, 'The Finding of the Saviour in the Temple', was on view at 'The Cups Hotel'.

Photographic art was progressing, and in January, 1865, Mr. James Barritt, photographer, Sir Isaac's Walk, was advertising 'a very pleasing and effective novelty in photographs — the Diamond Cameo Portraits, presenting the physiognomy of the subject in four distinct aspects; full face, right and left three quarter, and profile — in four oval medallions on one carte; and, by a process of embossing added, bringing out a very beautiful stereoscopic effect'.

Two important names in Colchester's history date back to the sixties.

Davey, Paxman & Co., a firm of ironmongers and engineers, began in 1865 first in the High Street and later in Culver Street. It made steam engines and agricultural machinery.

The other name was B. R. Cant, of St. John Street's Nurseries, and in July, 1868, they gave a show of cut roses at the Cups Hotel, and 'a finer or more extensive assortment of blooms it would be impossible to imagine'.

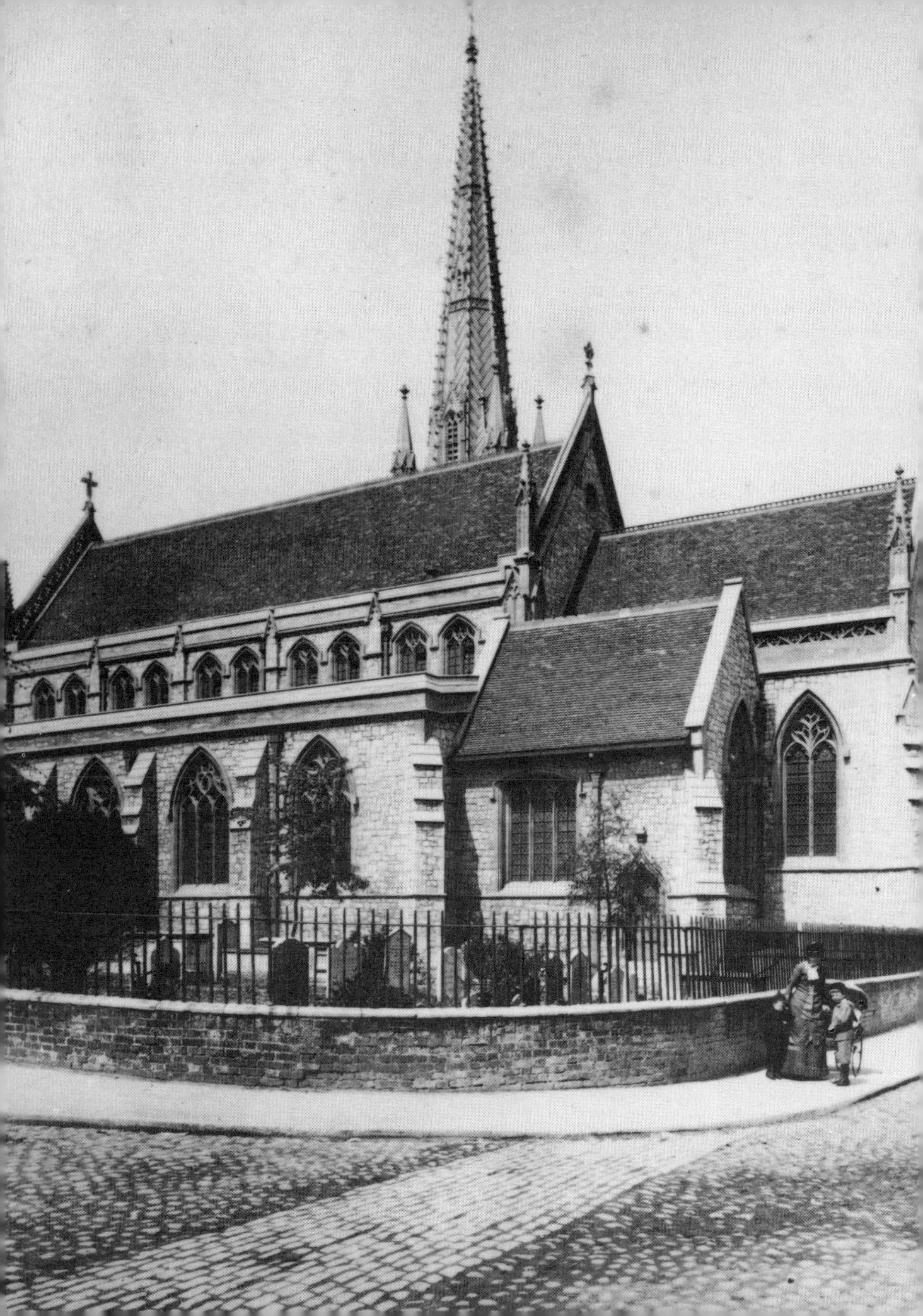

THE SEVENTIES

After the building of the Cavalry Barracks in the previous decade, it is interesting to note that in March, 1870, a small detachment of the Royal Artillery arrived in the town.

It was obvious that Colchester was again going to have a military flavour, and in September, 1873, a Soldiers' Home was re-opened in Osborne Street by Miss Daniells of the Soldiers' Mission, Aldershot. It had a reading room, library, smoking room and a refreshment bar. In August, three years later, a new Soldiers' Home was erected in Queen Street.

The average Colcestrian was probably not overconcerned about the welfare of soldiers, but they did enjoy listening to military bands. The band of the 108th regiment played from four to five o'clock in the Abbey Field, every Tuesday afternoon during June, 1877.

There were also weekly concerts given in the Castle Gardens by the 105th Light Infantry.

The following programme of military band music was given by the band of the 1-10th Regiment in the Castle Gardens in May 1879:

1. Marche. Belle Mahone. Young.
2. Selection. La Grande Duchesse de Gerolstein. Offenbach.
3. Valse. An der Schönen Blauen Donau. Strauss.
4. Selection. Robin Hood. Macfarren.
5. Mazurka. Gertrude. Heinsdorff.
6. Galop Militaire. Gallant and Gay. Carroll.

Left:
The Church of St. Nicholas and St. Runwald. When St. Runwald's was demolished the two churches were joined together. The new church of St. Nicholas was one of Sir Gilbert Scott's last designs. The old nave and chancel became the north aisle and chapel of a fine building which had a prominent spire — AC.

Right:
The tower of St. Mary's at the Wall Church. The original very poor structure of bricks was removed in 1871 and the present church was built from the designs of Sir Arthur Blomfield. The cottages have now been demolished — AC.

St. James Church on East Hill in the eighteen eighties. In 1855 a very fine reredos was erected to the late George Round, Esq. and the stone font was presented by Mrs. Round in memory of her husband — AC.

In October, 1875, the military authorities deplored damage to young trees planted on the Abbey Field.

'The Essex Standard', in March 1871, informed its readers that a new rectory was to be erected for St. Mary's-at-the-Walls Church. A year later the old church was pulled down and restored.

Several residents on the east side of the town formed a committee in October, 1871 to place a clock in St. James' church tower. Scaffolding had already been erected for repairs to the tower. The clock was to be an eight-day turret clock by Dent and Co., with one dial facing East Hill. It would strike the hours on a large bell to be erected on the top of the tower.

Three years later, in June, the St. Peter's church clock was regulated to Greenwich (Railway) time to agree with the clock at the Post Office. This also applied to the clock on the Corn Exchange.

In April, 1872, the Colchester and Essex Hospital had a new clock supplied by Mr. J. C. Hopwood, to replace the old one.

Sir Gilbert Scott, accompanied by the Rector, inspected St. Nicholas Church on February 8th, 1874 and promised to furnish the designs for the future church and to superintend their execution. By the following July the building of the new church was in progress and, on the Bank Holiday Monday, anyone could inspect it between the hours of ten o'clock in the morning and five o'clock in the evening. Two months later, the ancient, ruined church was being removed. On September 22nd. the clock, by which the old church was know as "The Dial Church", was taken down. In May, 1879, the new church had a permanent organ.

In November, 1875, there was a project to remove the gateway of St. Peter's Church. It was substituted by 'a suitable pair of ornamental gates, surmounted by circular gas lamps'. The old wall that ran parallel to the street was lowered, and faced with Portland cement. A handsome iron palisading on stone coping was also erected.

There was also much demolition to the little Church of St. Runwald in March, 1878. In that month little remained except the massive north and south walls.

By January, 1879, there was on display at Messrs. Benham and Harrison's Library, High Street, a view of the new Church of St. Nicholas and St. Runwald's by a 'clergyman resident in the neighbourhood'. In the same year a southern

Some Colchester Photographers.

Top right:
James Barritt, Northlight House, Colchester — AC.

Middle:
Joseph Higby, Photographer, 3, Chapel Street — AC.

Bottom right:
G. Stringer, 7 Chapel Street — AC.

St. Runwald's Church and Middle Row. St. Runwald's occupied an important position in the High Street. It was demolished in 1878. The houses known as Middle Row were destroyed some twenty years before — AC.

aisle was added to St. Paul's Church. The Rev. S. Baring Gould described this church as, 'a small, modern church at the bottom of the hill upon which Colchester is built'. He preached there occasionally to a 'congregation of railway porters, small tradesmen and artisans'.

By June, 1871, a committee was appointed by the Town Council for certain improvements to the Town Hall. Arrangements were made for the general repair of the assembly room, council chamber, ante-rooms, the committee rooms, the two courts, etc., work was also carried out on the exterior.

Four years later, for a few days in August, the Town Hall displayed 'the gem of the international art exhibition of 1871'. For one sixpence admission, between the hours of eleven o'clock and five o'clock, one could admire the celebrated picture of Lady Godiva by J. Van Lerius, President of the Royal Academy of Arts, Antwerp.

At that time, Colchester had a distinguished artist, Mr. Edward Ladell, son of a coachbuilder on East Hill. His still life pictures won him a world wide reputation, and during his life time he was regularly represented at the Royal Academy. For instance, in May, 1876, his picture, 'Fruit and Still Life', was on display there.

Colchester was then, as it is now, a rich inspiration for photographers as well as artists. One exhibition in July, 1878, featured 'Beautiful views of the town lately photographed by Mr. A. Seeley, of Richmond, including the castle in its present improved aspect, the High Street without St. Runwald's Church, St. Peter's Church, St. Botolph's Church, St. Mary's Church, St. Nicholas Church, Holy Trinity Church, and several views of the Barracks and Camp'.

In May, 1871, under the Bank Holiday Bill, banks closed on Whit Monday. Just over a year later in August, to relieve the dull appearance caused by the closing of all business premises, the Mayor directed that the Borough flags should be flown at the Town Hall. It was also suggested that those who had flags should display them.

By June, 1878, a Bank Holiday entertainment was provided for the public in the form of an alfresco fete in a meadow on the Harwich road, 'with walking and singing matches, a military tug of war, nigger performances, the inevitable peep shows, and rifle galleries'.

The following year the new bank of Messrs. Round and Green, started in the High Street in July.

As early as May, 1871, the Cattle Market was gradually becoming one of the largest stock markets in the Eastern Counties.

There was an election on a busy Market Day in November, 1879. Both parties were astir making arrangements long before the poll opened at nine o'clock. The town was 'all bustle and excitement, until seven when the poll was declared. Cabs and other vehicles carried voters and requested votes. Their drivers wore the distinguishing "blue" and "yellow" colours. The day did not conclude without one or two street fights, the result of inebriation, over zealousness, or both'.

A busy High Street scene during an election in the nineties — CM.

The postal service was developed in the seventies. By November, 1871, two telegraph wires were erected over the housetops from the telegraph offices in the High Street and St. John's Street, to St. Botolph's Station. They were in 'full working order to the several postal telegraphs in the Tendring Hundred'.

In March, 1874, a roomy new postal and telegraph office had been built in Head Street. On March 24th it replaced the office at the top of North Hill, and business commenced. The old office was closed and all messages were despatched from the new office. Within a few weeks, the money order and postal business was also transferred there from the High Street.

To compensate in some measure for the removal of the office, a pillar letter-box was erected at the hall-keeper's entrance to the Town Hall in August, 1875. The times of collection were:

Weekdays 8.55 am, 1.40 pm, 3.30 pm, 9.25 pm.
Sundays (once only) 9.25 pm.

Two years later, times by which telegrams could be despatched on Sundays from the Colchester Post Office were changed. Instead of from seven o'clock to nine o'clock they were sent from five o'clock to six o'clock.

In February, 1879, these were the times of Colchester Telegraph and Postal Office town deliveries: 7.15 am, 11.30 am and 6.30 pm. The letter box was cleared for the first delivery at 6 am, second delivery 11.15 am, and third delivery 6.10 pm. On Sunday, Good Friday and Christmas Day only the first delivery was made. There was a delivery to callers at 7.15 am, 11.30 am, 2.30 pm, 4.50 pm, and 6.30 pm.

The Tendring Hundred Railway, it was thought in May 1874, was made as effective and serviceable as the neighbourhood through which it passed deserved. Colchester trade had previously been hindered by the distance of the Hythe Goods Station from the town centre.

It should also be noted that in 1876, Davey, Paxman & Co. was established at the Hythe as the Standard Iron Works. By this time they were well known as makers of boilers and steam engines. The ironworks depended more on the railway for coal and transport rather than Colchester's port.

Top right:
High Street in the eighteen eighties, looking east. It once ran on to pass through the western wall of the Balkerne Gate. In earlier times parts were otherwise named. At its western end 'Cornhill', towards its eastern end 'King Street' and at its extreme east 'Frere' (or Friars Street) after the monastery of the Grey Friars. Note the Essex and Suffolk fire office built on the site of the Dutch Bay Hall — AC.

Bottom right:
High Street looking west in the eighteen eighties. This is after the demolition of St. Runwald's Church. Note the George Hotel, another important Colchester inn. The Victorian Town Hall can just about be seen on the horizon — AC.

Below:
Head Street, circa 1870. Commercial premises included Henry Aggio, piano manufacturers, Mattacks the booksellers, Joseph Parish, portrait and animal painter and drawing master and William Frederick Allen, tailor and woollen draper at the top of High Street and Head Street. The important inn, The Fleece, was owned by Thomas Bolton — National Monuments Record.

Another form of transport, the bicycle, had its adherents, and the Colchester Bicycle Club had its headquarters at the George Hotel.

In March, 1870, under the Colchester Improvement Act, tenders were received for supplying and laying York pavement, granite kennelling and other work on the footpaths of the town. The large work of paving was given to a London firm despite the fact there had been local stonemasons out of work all the winter.

The Corporation, in 1875, 'became the sole sanitary body of the town, for lighting, paving, drainage and peace and quiet'.

Four years later, in May, there was an improvement in street lighting when the gasworks company placed some new lamps at the west end of High Street, near the Corn Exchange. 'The lamps were lighted for the first time on Thursday evening, and though the night was miserably wet, a goodly number of people visited the neighbourhood of their erection, and expressed general satisfaction at the innovation'.

By October the same year, handsome new buildings were nearly ready in the High Street. These were to replace those destroyed by fire in the February of 1878. The new property, 'of lofty and commanding appearance', was occupied in the centre by Mr. Comer, a draper, and those on either side were to be occupied by Messrs., Pocock Bros., and Mr. R. Parsons.

THE SWA
INN
EASTERN COUNTIES HAT DEPOT.
IPSWICH NORWICH
GREEN & Co
YARMOUTH

In March, 1877, the Colchester Gasworks Company remodelled their general works, with a new retort house, cool stores and other buildings. Two years later the Corporation purchased the undertaking of the waterworks which were immediately commenced and improved.

From about 1845 until 1875 the field boundaries of London Road were gradually partly overlaid by plots and streets of 'handsome villas'.

Of the larger town houses, a typical Victorian mansion was 'Scarletts', Old Heath, that was occupied in the sixties by F. B. Philbrook, an attorney and first Town Clerk to the reformed Corporation. It was described in an advertisement in 1877, as follows:

'The House is well-situate. dry and on gravel. It contains 3 Reception-Rooms of good dimensions, Smoking-Room, 4 Principal Bedrooms, 2 large Servants-Rooms, Bathroom, with service for hot, cold, and shower baths, two WC's, kitchens, cellars and usual out offices. Attached are stabling, carriage house, gardener's cottage, flower and kitchen garden, orchard, hot-house, green-house, propogating house, farmery, and agricultural buildings, uplaid and low meadowland well watered. The whole area is about 18 acres. Good railway accommodation. Foxhounds in neighbourhood. Capitally placed for yachting, wildfowl, and fishing'.

There was however, one drawback to this otherwise healthy town. this being the impurity of the Colne which was

St. Leonard's Church in the eighteen eighties. The church was damaged in the 1884 earthquake and about £600 was spent on restoration — AC.

considered 'fearfully detrimental', and thought to be the cause of intermittent fevers in the lower parts of the parishes of St. Peter, St. James, and St. Leonard. In January, 1876, there were a few cases of scarlet fever, but these were not of a serious character.

The new Wesleyan Schools opened in Culver Street in June 1870. They had been 'erected in a most substantial manner by Messrs. Shepherd Brothers, contractors, St. John's Street'.

A year later, in November, an evening school for the 'working classes' was opened in Water Lane, Middleborough. It was open on Monday and Tuesday evenings at seven o'clock, and was especially intended for those residing in the St. Paul's district of Lexden, but young men from any other part of the town were invited to attend.

On New Year's Day, 1872, Mrs. Laver, wife of the House Surgeon, assisted by several ladies gave the children of the Colchester Union their customary treat. The treat took the form of a Christmas tree, 'which afforded much gratification and amusement'.

Her Majesty's Inspectors report on the Ragged Schools was published in April, three years later, and read as follows:

'Central. Boys. The order and organisation of 342 boys, does great credit to Mr. Harris. The instruction also is very satisfactory. Girls. This school is conducted with the greatest care. The instruction is most efficiently imparted. The sewing is also very well executed. St. James Branch. This school does credit to its teacher for the order, discipline, and instruction, which are well maintained. The sewing also and cutting out are skilfully executed'.

A football match between old boys of the Colchester Royal Grammar School took place on the school playground on Boxing Day, 1875. After the match the participants dined together at the George Hotel, under the presidency of the Headmaster, (the Rev. C. L. Acland).

Mrs. George Round treated the children of St. James Infants School, East Street, in January 1876.

'131 children ranging from two to eleven, looking the perfection of health, cleanliness and good order, assembled in the School-Room, under the direction of their governess, Miss Green, and her assistant, and at one o'clock, grace having been said, smoking hot plum puddings were brought in, and disposed of with almost magical celerity by the youngsters'.

By 1876, the town council had set up a School Attendance Committee.

More visitors came to the museum in the castle, in 1870. In May, 1869, there were 648 visitors, and in May 1870, there were 947. There were 28,000 visitors in 1872, and in the following year the Rev. C. L. Acland was appointed the Honorary Curator.

From time to time the museum received contributions, for instance, in February, 1871, 'The contributions during the past month have not been so numerous as usual, but they include a most valuable addition to the Natural History Department in the shape of Indian and other snakes in a most perfect state of preservation'.

The Early Closing Movement continued. The great majority of tradesmen in May, 1870, decided to close their establishments at 5 o'clock on Thursday afternoons in the summer months. This was doubtless, 'greatly appreciated both by employers and those employed'. The last closing day of the season was in September, and on that Thursday a very pleasant time was spent in dancing at 'an invited party of assistants of both sexes.'

Part of the castle used as a museum — CM.

In the summer months of 1875 a good number of establishments closed at five o'clock but this was by no means general, except among the drapers.

The following closed at two o'clock on Thursdays in the summer months of 1876. Banks, bazaars, bootmakers, china dealers, clothiers, drapers, hatters, jewellers, leather cutters, milliners, pawnbrokers and piano warehouses.

These did not close until the evening: booksellers, butchers, brush makers, carriage builders, chemists, confectioners, corn chandlers, coopers, fishmongers, grocers, gun makers, greengrocers, hairdressers, harness makers, ironmongers, plumbers, oil and colourmen, printers, tobacconists, upholsterers, wine merchants and woollen drapers.

This was the result of proposing to close at two o'clock instead of five o'clock.

For those with money the Christmas shops were always attractive. In December, 1872, for instance, there was, 'a very large and prime show of meat, the grocers present an almost endless variety of fruit, etc. and the poulterers also provide with the time-honoured Christmas bird, etc'.

The Theatre Royal was opened for one Monday night in March, 1873, by the Misses MacCambridge. The pieces played were, 'The Flowers of the Forest', and the burlesque of 'Kenilworth'. In the latter the Amazonian Ballet, from 'Babel and Bijou' was introduced.

In October, 1876, Flotow's Comic Opera, in three acts, L'Ombre (The Phantom), was performed by the French Opera Company. 'The music is of the most exquisite description, and is considered the best of the author's productions. It was rendered by highly talented artistes... with full costumes and grand effects'.

In the same month popular military amateurs appeared, and the local press commented, 'When Amateur Thespians connected with the Garrison don the the socks and buskin — our theatre instead of presenting a beggarly array of empty benches is always filled, and most of the leading families in town and neighbourhood attend'.

In 1875 there has been a creditable attempt to portray, Hamlet.

However, at most times, the theatre was not considered respectable, and in the following month Colchester Theatre was surveyed, 'with a view of being converted into a Soldiers' Home'.

The Indian Famine of 1877 caused much suffering and Colcestrians wanted to support a national fund to relieve those afflicted. On October 11th, under the patronage of the Mayor, Thomas Moy, the 'Officers and Ladies' of the 64th Regiment presented, 'The Balance of Comfort' and 'The Bonnie Fishwife'.

The Theatre Royal was never converted into a Soldiers' Home. In March, 1878, the Nunn Bros. — Edwin, Henry and John, well known amateur Colcestrian actors, purchased the theatre, and despite their many mistakes, owned it until 1889.

They spent a considerable sum on repairs, improvements, decoration and in making the auditorium more comfortable. They also kept their intention of providing Colchester with more frequent and varied theatrical entertainment.

In 1878 at the 'Thespian Temple at Colchester', the highlights included the Court Minstrels, Mr. and Mrs. German Reed's Entertainment assisted by Corney Grain, and Mr. Howard Paul and his amusing concert and entertainment from the Alexandra Palace.

J. L. Toole advertised as 'the most popular comedian of the day'. He came to Colchester in 1879 and 1882 — AC.

In the following year, Colcestrians enjoyed a pantomime 'Cinderella' with its notable Palace and Transformation scene, J. L. Toole (the most popular comedian of his day) and full company in 'A Fool and His Money', by Mr. A. G. Vance, the Matthew Minstrels, the Charles Wyndham Company in the celebrated comedies, 'Pink Dominoes' and 'Truth', and the D'Oyly Carte Opera Company in 'H.M.S. Pinafore'.

It is interesting to note the local press comment on the latter: 'As a literary production, perhaps, not much can be said in its favour, but still it is pleasantly written, and the good humoured satire on First Lords without nautical experience, etc., is very mirth-provoking, while Mr. Sullivan's music is of the most fascinating character'.

The Public Hall provided alternative entertainment. In November, 1870, Miss Emma Stanley portrayed, 'The Seven Ages of Woman', the last 'age' was especially admired. Also, 'with marvellous rapidity she assumed the native costumes of Italian, Spanish, Turkish, Scottish, Swiss and French character, and sang a melody in each language'.

That extraordinary troupe of little people, called the 'Tom Thumb Company', came the following May. This consisted of Tom Thumb and wife, Commodore Nutt and Mrs. Minnie Warren. The latter charmingly sang several songs; and Commodore Nutt's comicalities called forth roars of laughter.

In September Colchester audiences were delighted by Miss Lydia Howard, aged seven years, described as a 'wonderfully gifted little actress and singer'. On Wednesday evening she portrayed no less than eight characters in 'the most perfect manner, and yet with artless and childish simplicity'.

In January, 1872, Mr. Albert Jones, author of the celebrated, 'Humours of Bartlemy Fair', gave an entertainment. He was also a clever mimic and ventriloquist. His entertainment, lasting nearly two hours, was entitled 'A Night in London, or an Evening's Amusement with the World's Celebrity'.

Three years later, in January, Mrs. Fanny Edwards (Mrs. Harry Clifton) visited Colchester with her Concert and Operetta Company.

The Public Hall was the scene for Strange and Wilson's Spectral Opera Company in May, 1876. The main attraction was 'Faust' with Gounod's music.

In the following year, Mr. Charles Hallé played there on a Broadwoods concert grand and Madame Norman Nerunda played on her famous Ernst violin.

Colchester Football Club started in October 1873.

A skating rink was built, only to be used as hall three years later. It was 131 feet long and sixty feet wide.

By 1877 there was some entertainment at the Rink. The Jubilee Singers sang some quaint slave songs. Messrs. Selbini and Villon gave daily velocipede and acrobatic performances. Another act was Mr. J. Atherton and his performing dogs.

In 1878 there were Chinese Bicycle Skaters, and the Imperial Russian Skaters and Pantomimists, Mr. and Mrs. F. Ryder, Mr. C. S. Ryder, and Mlle. Clairette — 'Their skating is both graceful and scientific, and their comic sketches are exceedingly clever and amusing'. Also at the skating rink in the same year was an exhibition of a, 'large number of cooking stoves, photometric and other apparatus. . .'

Franconi's Circus came to Colchester in August, 1871. 'The feats of horsemanship appeared to be much appreciated, and Loto, "the Flying Lady", a new feature at this circus was greeted with enthusiastic applause at each daring leap she took across the ring. The clowns were very amusing, and the performing dogs were exceedingly clever'.

Six years later, after a most gorgeous parade through the town, Sanger's Circus was located at the Cattle Market.

Animals played a part in the life of Victorian Colchester. On one August Thursday afternoon, 1870, 'a horse, the property of Messrs. Davey, Paxman and Davey, which was at work in their yard at Maldon Road, took fright at the whistle of one of the engines, and bolted off at a furious pace. In its course it frightened a pony in front of a newly erected house, and thus still attached to the cart, cleared it. It then commenced kicking and was not extricated till it had committed considerable damage. The other horse proceeded at a sharp pace up Crouch Street and Head Street, and was eventually secured in High Street without having occasioned much damage'.

Three years later, on one Monday morning in August, a well known horse dealer was driving into the town, when he had occasion to get out of his trap to speak to a friend in

St. John's Street 1895. It was formerly called 'Gutter Street' or Lane, from an open gutter or ditch which originally ran down the middle of it. To the left is the quaint Scheregate and to the left of the Brewers Arms is Vineyard Street. This was so named about 1854 from a supposed vineyard said to have existed near by. To the right of the Brewers Arms is Osborne Street named after Thomas Osborne whose brewery was near by. Up to about 1860 it was waste land — EL.

Crouch Street. During this time a hare escaped from his vehicle. 'The street was soon in considerable commotion and an exciting chase took place'. The hare was coursed up and down and in and out of several shops, eventually being captured by a second-hand furniture dealer living in St. John's Street.

'In February, 1879, at about five o'clock one Tuesday, a furious bull was at large in St. John's Street. It lifted a child from the ground, and rushed at a horse. Fortunately some occupants of the cart prevented in from doing any more harm. The bull then made its way to St. John's Green'.

The Colchester Poor Relief Committee, in February, 1870, distributed five hundred tickets to the poor of St. Peter's parish. There were less vagrants in the town that year; 30th September, 1869 . . . 1,901 and 8th June, 1870 . . . 1,201.

There was a marked absence of crime during January 1871, which, 'especially remembering the weather of late, reflects the greatest possible credit upon the town'.

On New Year's Day, 1878 about forty of the poor of St. Mary's parish, chiefly widows and widowers, 'were supplied with a substantial dinner of hot beef, vegetables and bread, the cost of which was defrayed by a few benevolent ladies and gentlemen of the parish'.

Another good influence was the Temperance Movement whose teetotal preachings continued to make the Age somewhat more sober, and, at least, aware of the evils of drink.

As a safeguard, in 1879, a volunteer fire brigade was formed by twelve men. The superintendent was the chief constable. By the aid of voluntary subscriptions from the Essex and Suffolk Insurance Society, a steam fire engine was purchased.

The town experienced a severe gale and intense cold in February, 1870, and 'clouds of dust which continually rose into the air being at times almost blinding'.

Five years later, in November, floods overflowed all the quays, and the basements of most of the houses along the banks. Several lighters had been left high and dry upon the quays, and had to be lifted by cranes into the river.

THE EIGHTIES

Colchester's most momentous event of the eighteen eighties, in fact of all its Victorian era, was the earthquake of 1884. This alarming occurrence took place at twenty minutes past nine on April 22nd, and lasted several seconds. 'The ground was convulsed from one end of the town to the other, houses were shaken to their foundations, bells were set a-ringing, pictures dislodged from the walls, vases and ornaments on tables and cheffories overturned and thrown down, and hundreds of chimneys wrecked'.

Such an unprecedented event resulted in consternation. All rushed into the streets expecting to see visible signs of the earthquake. There was panic. Women shrieked in terror and strong men were 'utterly unnerved and paralysed'.

The lofty and elegant spire of Lion Walk Congregational Church had been overturned and almost demolished.

At first it was thought that the Dynamites had destroyed the Garrison magazines. Crowds, thinking the gasometers had been blown up, flocked to the gasworks. Fire Brigade men rushed through the street to put out fires at Maidenburgh Street, the Rev. Coley's house in Roman Road, and at Miss Viney's on East Hill.

Many of the old tenements suffered most, and there was damage in Magdalen Street, Barrack Street, Artillery Street, and other thoroughfares in the Hythe. Streets were strewn with debris.

The Duke of York Inn was among many places affected. At the workhouse three chimneys had crashed

Left:
A scene after the earthquake of 1884. The shock caused widespread superficial damage in Colchester, and brought down some of the steeple of Lion Walk Congregational Church — AC.

North Hill. Leads north from the top of High Street. Together with North Station Road was known as North Street up to the sixteenth century and perhaps later. To the right is St. Peter's Church, the town church. The tower, bold in appearance but somewhat ungainly, had an illuminated dial added to it in 1866. The interior was improved in 1869. To the left is the premises of William Robert Simkin. cabinet and chair maker, upholsterer, undertaker, furnisher, etc. — EL.

through the roof. Other damage was at North Hill, Eld Lane, Scheregate and St. John's Street. In fact few houses escaped some kind of damage.

In the various schools the children had only just assembled. The shock was so terrible and caused so much alarm and panic, that the scholars were at once allowed to return home. Persons wishing to send telegrams besieged the Post Office. Nearly a hundred messages were sent within the hour.

In the previous August the town had experienced such thunder-storms that had not been known for at least twenty five years. Water remained about three feet deep in Maldon Road. Many of the lower rooms here, and in Butt Road were flooded.

'The telephonic wire communications between the publishing offices of 'The Essex Telegraph' in Head Street with the printing works in East Stockwell Street was repeatedly struck, and made the bells in connection with the apparatus ring'.

On December 1st, 1886, the town crier, James Simpson, walked the streets until about three o'clock in the morning, crying,

'O yes! O yes! O yes!
Cold December has set in,
Poor people's backs are clothed thin,
The trees are bare,
The birds are mute,
A pot and toast would very well suit
Past 12 o'clock on a cold and starlight morning,
Good morning, masters and mistresses to you all,
I hope you will all live to see
Queen Victoria's Jubilee'.

In 'The Essex Standard' for July 2nd, 1887, there were two illustrations of Colchester celebrating this historic event. One picture shows the night illuminations in the High Street.

The other was a rough pen and ink sketch depicting the children's procession. Over five thousand children took part in the tableaux representing personalities and scenes in the old town's long history. An amateur photographer Mr. Shenstone, took some 'admirable instantaneous photographs of the procession'. He sold these for a shilling each, and the proceeds went to a local charity.

In the previous issue there was an illustration of the proposed new Town Hall, 'for although it was rejected as a

Magdalen Street 1895. Joins St. Botolph's Corner and Barrack Street. An unfashionable part of town. Anciently called Heth Street leading to the Hythe. In about 1860 called Commercial Road. Note to the right part of Military Road as far as Winnock Road. This was called Hog Lane — EL.

Jubilee Commemoration, it had not disappeared from party politics'.

The Jubilee decorations in High Street equalled those of any London Street. Bunting and evergreens were frequently used and, 'the interesting old front of the Red Lion presented a gay appearance with flags and flowers and Chinese lanterns'.

Many patriotic words were portrayed — such as, 'Queen Victoria whom God preserves' and 'Jubilee of Our Beloved Queen'.

Food, groceries, etc. were distributed to the poor. The Abbey Field was the scene of a review of about two thousand three hundred soldiers, athletic sports, and a bonfire.

At the Children's Treat, each child received a Jubilee medal, a bag containing six ounces of cake, a plain bun, a currant bun, and a good supply of tea.

The Essex and Suffolk Fire Office on the occasion of the Queen's Jubilee, 21st June, 1887 — AC.

Decorations to celebrate the Queen's Jubilee in 1887. This scene is at the corner of Queen Street and High Street. To the left is All Saint's Church — CM.

The celebrations also included fireworks and illuminations. At the Town Hall there was a small star. Nine windows were filled with transparencies, the centre being a crown and V.R.

Several famous people visited Colchester during this decade. In February, 1883, Prince Leopold, Duke of Albany, K.G., visited the town for a Grand Masonic meeting, in which he presided over the installment of Lord Broke.

Five years later, in June, His Royal Highness, the Duke of Cambridge, K.G., etc., Field Marshall commanding in chief of the Army, came to inspect the troops of the Garrison, and, 'to perform the pleasing ceremony of presenting the new colours to the 1st. Durham Light Infantry'.

Prince Albert Victor, eldest son of the Prince of Wales, in July, 1889, opened a Grand Bazaar, in aid of 'The Church of England's Soldier's Institute'.

Mr. Oscar Wilde, in March, 1884, gave two lectures at the Town Hall. The first was about 'The House Beautiful', and the other, 'Personal Impressions of America'. Wilde caused no great sensation. 'The first lecture delivered by this well known gentleman was listened to with considerable interest by a considerable auditory, but the attendance was small in the evening. The lecturer's quaint view of men and manners were expressed in characteristic style. A good deal of common sense and much sentiment was stated in a manner which interested without creating much solid impression'.

Doctor Barnado lectured at the New Corn Exchange on March 8th, 1887. His subject was 'Work for Christ among the Waifs and Strays of Our Streets'. The advertisment announced, 'Five little boys from one of the Orphan Homes will play selections of music during the evening on their sweet peal of sixty bells'. At that time the Homes were helping one thousand nine hundred waifs and later Colcestrians sent a cheque for £63.12s.1d. Dr. Barnado again spoke at the Corn Exchange on December 17th, 1889.

The military sometimes caused a disturbance. In May, 1880, shortly before midnight on one Friday, some artillerymen were causing a fracas in High Street. They were eventually secured by the police with great difficulty. Shortly afterwards, another mêlée occurred in Head Street. This was originally caused by two artillerymen attacking a sergeant in the Hussars. The men were extremely violent and it took several constables to get them to the barracks.

In the same year, in October, the Lieut.-General commanding regretted that certain Volunteers had, 'the improper and unsoldier-like habit of smoking in the street when under arms and proceeding to the place of assembly of their regiments, and also when walking in uniform'.

In December, 1880, military bands in the town thoroughfares became a subject of controversy. Certain people complained that the bands were a cause of 'many horse and carriage accidents and a risk to life and limb and the loss of valuable property'. The military authorities had had strong representations regarding the, 'undesirability of music in the streets'.

Moreover, 'Many ladies and gentlemen were afraid to drive into town, and trade suffered in consequence. Vehicle drivers had enough already to bear with traction engines, locomotives, bicycles, etc.' However, military bands had their supporters. They were all right in the correct place. There was the splendid band of the 50th Regiment that played at the Camp on summer evenings. Delightful military music was sometimes heard at the Theatre. For several summer Sundays the band of the 13th Hussars played between 11 o'clock and 12 o'clock in the morning, and 9 o'clock and 10 o'clock in the evening. In January, 1886, the weekly promenade concerts, given by the band of the Essex Regiment at the New Corn Exchange, became increasingly popular.

There was, in January, 1889, a farewell banquet to Sir Evelyn Wood, Bart., VC, KCB, etc., who had held command of troops in the Eastern District.

In 1882 Colchester was confronted with another kind of army. 'The War Cry', the organ of the Salvation Army published this account in June of that year.

'The Salvation Army opening of Colchester, from Major Blasy.

Capture of Burglars — 110 prisoners'.

'Saturday, met in Cattle Market, music playing, people rushing. First shots aroused the prince of darkness, but told well upon his soldiers; thousands in the march; rink packed, powerful service'.

'Sunday, seven o'clock Knee drill, people wept all round. At ten multitudes in the streets. After a telling march we opened fire inside, and very soon four hell-bound captives were taken to Jesus, who broke their fetters and set them free; two of them were between 60 and 70 years of age. Afternoon, about 4,000 in the march. Captured en route two burglars and conjurers, brought them with us to the Barracks; they fell at the feet of Jesus, confessed they had been getting their living by thieving all their lives — they burnt their bag of tools and tricks'.

'At night the King's message was with irresistable power; crying for mercy, 106 volunteered from the ranks of the devil to serve King Jesus'.

Captain Polly Perken.

The following April, General William Booth, the militant head of the Salvation Army, paid his second visit to the town. He was driven to the residence of Mr. Edward Marriage, in East Hill. Subsequently he took part in the usual evening service at the Rink, and also on a Sunday afternoon. 'His appeals to the unconverted were strengthened with frequent narratives, mostly taken from the 'Army' experiences'.

In 1885, the Salvation Army introduced a 'decided novelty' to their service, with the 'Blind Brigade' from

London. Staff-Captain Bennett, known as 'The Black Prince' was in command. The 'soldiers' under him consisted of 'Blind Jimmy' with his concertina' 'Blind Mark' with his banjo; and 'Blind Willie' with his Bible. All the members wore distinctive jackets, of a white material with broad sashes.

In the following May, Miss Eva Booth, daughter of the General, took part in the services. Three years later, in November, her father was welcomed with great excitement when the Salvation Army place of worship was re-opened — 'cheers upon cheers were raised, and hats, scarfs and handkerchiefs waved in the air. In his speech he said that there were now 2,728 in the camps, and that they had been able to help the poor'.

More conventional worshippers probably complained about St. Peter's Church bells on the dawning of New Year's day, 1883, for, 'At midnight they rang out their sacred diabolical peal, and their tintinnabulations, added to the tramp of the hurrying feet of worshippers returning from watch-services, must have sorely tried the tempers of would-be slumberers'.

'The Essex Telegraph' in May, 1881, published this prophetic comment about a Public Garden in Colchester.

'We have always maintained that the ground around the castle should be retained, as it was in ancient days for the recreation of the inhabitants'.

However, the first public park was the Recreation Ground, released from the military authorities in 1885. The formal opening took place at four o'clock on a May Thursday, and subsequently the Mayor and Corporation dined at the George Hotel.

In September, 1881, the need was also pointed out for more public seats, especially along the Lexden Road. Nurse-maids allowed children to sit on the damp grass, and tired adults sometimes did the same. At a time of agricultural depression in North Essex, the Essex Agricultural Show was, in June, 1889, held at Lexden Park with, 'its beautiful grounds with choice foliage and the beautiful trees always at their best.'

A complete inspection of the town wall was made in the winter of 1886 and repairs put in hand. A resolution was passed that no building in future would be allowed to be erected upon or against the wall.

A scene at Hythe Hill about the turn of the century — AC.

In February, 1881, the New Sewage Works was started. The starting point was Middleborough, 'where the contractors will work up Lexden Road in two or three sections, and the Hythe, whence the work will proceed up Hythe Hill, Magdalen Street, and Barrack Street. North Street and Station Road will be commenced in the Spring, and shortly afterwards the main sewer will be laid in the meadows between East Bridge and the Hythe, and will follow the course of the river'. Until 1881, when a bore was sunk, most of the water came from Clark's meadow.

With the construction of the New Sewage Works, drainage improved slowly with extensions to the old system. Since then many of the old sewers have been reconstructed.

The new water tower with its very red brick was, in July 1883, inspected by Mr. Rawlinson, the eminent engineer. He was very satisfied 'with the design and execution of this important understanding'. The water tower, one of the largest in England, with a tank holding 230,000 gallons, was officially opened in September.

The time of the postal telegraphs from April 1st, 1880, were 7 am-10 am on weekdays, and 7 am-10 am, and 5 pm-6 pm on Sundays. From March, 1885, there was an accelerated morning delivery of letters in the town.

In the following February it was observed that the custom of Valentine's Day, although still popular, appeared to be on the wane. Also in November, 1886, there were new pillar boxes in Creffield Road and Queen Street.

As far back as 1882, the town council considered supplying electric lighting in the borough. However, their application to the Board of Trade for a licence under the Electric lighting Act was withdrawn, and no more progress was made until the next decade.

There had been an experiment in electric lighting in September, 1882, by Evatt Saunders, the well known grocers and provision merchants of High Street, to illuminate their business premises. The gas lamps in comparison looked, 'yellow and dingy to the last degree'.

Three years later, Mr. O. E. Coope, M.P. in a letter to 'The Times' gave reference to the electric light at Berechurch Hall, 'The whole of the machinery and the conductors are working well. The expense is about the same as the previous year, being rather under what one would have to pay for gas, and the light is so charming, convenient and healthy, that after being accustomed to it, one is indisposed to sit in a room lighted in any other manner'.

Colchester kept in touch with the art world. On May 28th, 1885, the Colchester School of Art held an exhibition 'of paintings by Royal Academicians and other eminent artists, models from the Royal Architectural Institution, textile fabrics and lace, Corporation plate of various boroughs, Persian and European pottery'.

In the local world of education a Roman Catholic School was opened in 1883.

The following year saw the building of a New Corn Exchange, and in the October there was a banquet there to

Moot Hall, Corn Exchange 1884, and the important inn, The Cups Hotel, High Street — AC.

celebrate the re-opening of the Cups Hotel that had been rebuilt that year.

In 1883 there was a free Registry Office for young servants. This was at 15, St. Botolph's Street. 'First situations have been found for a considerable number of girls 12-16. An outfit is provided (if required) to be paid for afterwards out of the wages'.

Two years later a set of recreation rooms for young ladies 'employed in business', was established at 121, High Street.

In March, 1883, through the Early Closing Movement, the solicitors resolved to close their residential offices at 2 o'clock on Thursdays from April to September inclusive.

Six years later in September, a shop assistant hoped to get the tradesmen to close their business establishments at 5 o'clock on Thursdays during the winter months.

The Sudbury or South Annexe of the Eastern Counties Asylum was opened and inspected by the Duke of Norfolk on May 8th, 1889. Afterwards about two hundred lunched at the Recreation Hotel.

By the eighties, Bank Holiday pastimes included rail excursions to Walton on the Naze. In August, 1880, there was a children's excursion. Adults paid eightpence and

BUTTER

children paid fourpence. At least, 2,736 passengers were conveyed from St. Botolph's Station. Three years later, in January, the North Station was nearly destroyed when a fire broke out in the refreshment room.

As in ther seventies, omnibuses plied between the Cups Hotel and the Red Lion Hotel and the station, and also between the hotels and the first milestone of Lexden. On Sundays, in February, 1887, the omnibuses also saved people long walks by taking them to their places of worship. Also in February, 1887, the local branch of the R.S.P.C.A. announced a 'Horse Parade and Procession in Colchester'. 'It is proposed to offer prizes for the best turn out of team horses, van horses, horses used from trade purposes, cab horses, and donkeys'.

In January, 1883, there was a project to have trams in the town. It was supposed that the tramways would take all the length and breadth of Queen Street and St. Botolph's Street, but the service there would not be so frequent as that between North Station and the Town Hall. At that time, the proposed trams were considered beneficial, cheap, and a necessity. Apparently power had virtually been given to the promoters to construct the tramway line from North Station to All Saint's Church, terminating there, and commencing again at Plough Corner, continuing to the Hythe.

By April 21st, The Essex Telegraph published an order authorising the construction of tramways in the borough. Amongst many details, it stated that, 'The tramways may be used for the purpose of conveying passengers, animals, goods, minerals and parcels'. However, despite much enthusiasm in certain quarters, Colchester had no trams until 1904.

Cycling was becoming increasingly known, but cyclists were not always popular. One July Saturday in 1881, some cyclists were assaulted by roughs in St. Botolph's Street. A policeman told the cyclists that they had no business to be riding bicycles on Saturday night.

In July, the following year, the first County Meet was witnessed by Colcestrians.

'The science of bicycling is, of course, still in its infancy, and hence no previous display of these elegant, swift and noiseless machines, which have almost revolutionised previous methods of travel along our country roads, has been held in Colchester'. The meet therefore was a novelty.

Top Left:
St. Botolph's Street 1888, joins Queen Street and St. Botolph's Corner and Osborne Street. The photograph shows demolition work perhaps necessary as the result of the 1884 earthquake. Note the Eastern Company and J. H. Clamp, furnisher, pawnbroker, etc. It was a busy thoroughfare — EL.

Bottom Left:
St. Botolph's Street c. 1890. In 1895 it included upholsterers, ironmongers, bakers, a tobacconist, bootmakers, a plumber, confectioners, drapers, chemists, fruiterers, pork butcher, etc. Miss Bawtree was in charge of the Church of England Soldiers' Institute, N. Noble was in charge of the Marlboro' Head Hotel, and the Woolpack inn was owned by W. T. Pitt — EL.

Colcestrians turned out in thousands to welcome about two hundred riders who took part in the procession.

The chief hotels, especially those that are the headquarters of 'bicycle-touring clubs' and many leading establishments were decorated.

Two months later the annual race of the Colchester Bicycle Club was held on the Artillery Square, 'The weather was beautifully fine, and in consequence a large number of persons, including many ladies, witnessed the sports'.

From June 2nd until June 5th, 1886, there was a Congress of Cyclists. This included meetings at the Town Hall, visits to the museum and the castle, and an excursion through the 'Constable Country'.

There was 'capital skating' in the town in January, 1881. Without a doubt the most popular place was the Distillery Pond, where, 'many hundreds were to be seen flying about on steel blades'.

Six years later, in the same month, skating was enjoyed in Mr. Spalding's meadow and Knight's meadow, either side of North Bridge.

In that winter also, snow was cleared away from the streets under the superintendence of the Borough Surveyor. In addition to the sixty men employed there were a hundred and fifty extra men. Besides the usual Corporation waggons thirty five carts were used.

In August, 1883, Master Charles Brown, aged nine, showed 'extraordinary powers of shooting' at Reed Hall. Skilfully he broke glass balls thrown in the air. His other deeds included destroying the 'new invented clay pigeons'. Messrs. Agle and Frost thought Master Brown was worthy of being photographed.

The Temperance Movement continued to have its advocates. Mr. Asher Prior at the Band of Hope meeting in February 1885 pointed out that, 'whatever difference there might be with regard to the practice of total abstinence by adults, there could be little doubt as to its being the best thing for children'.

In April, 1880, the Volunteer Fire Brigade ordered a new steam fire engine. It cost £360 from a London firm. The fire engine had its first practice in September 'without the assistance of horses'. Half a dozen members of the Brigade took the engine from the engine house in West

Stockwell Street, running her easily down to the south side of St. Botolph's brewery'.

Three years later, in March, there appeared to be a fire epidemic in the town. There were three fires in eight days; one being a chimney at the residence of the Misses Box, Lexden Heath.

Saturday crowds welcomed Bostock and Wombwell's Menagerie in February, 1882. Their exhibition was on view in the evening and was 'patronised extensively'. At certain times lectures were given and the caged animals gave 'exciting performances'.

In Whitsun of the same year there was a Volunteer Fete at Reed Hall, with a showman, clown, music hall vocalists, swing boats, weighing machines, numerous stalls, and a firework display.

Sangers Circus entertained in Colchester in October, 1883. A fine brass band led a procession that included horses, ponies, elephants, dromedaries, camels and a hundred and twenty six employees. A handsome carriage driven by Mr. Burk was drawn by forty horses.

Poole's Diorama in January, 1885, gave Colcestrians at least a glimpse of other lands.

In the eighties pastoral plays performed at the Holly Trees became popular. In July, 1886, Miss Alexas Leighton from the Lyceum promised to play the principal lady's part.

Also in the late Victorian times Matinee Musicales were popular at the Drill Hall. In April, 1888, the programmes included Miss Annie Roberts (from the Royal College), Mr. Hayden Coffin (who had not visited Colchester for a long time), Master Ham, the celebrated boy from the Temple Church, and several others. But the principal attraction was the appearance of Miss Fortescue, 'the professional beauty who has been so much talked of in Society this year or so'.

Also in Colchester in 1888, a 'Stag Hunt' was the highlight of the Olympia Hippodrome and Circus at the Cattle Market, and a firework display in North Street included the playing of two military bands, and concluded with a 'Wonderful Pictorial and Pyrotechnical Representation of the Bombardment of Alexandria!

The eighteen eighties saw the rise and fall of the Nunn Bros. régime at the Theatre Royal. Amongst their many extremely popular shows, their particular favourites included the D'Oyly Carte Opera Company in Gilbert and Sullivan's,

Mr. C. Hayden-Coffin came to Colchester in 1888 — AC.

Miss Nellie Farren came in 1885 with her comedy and burlesque Company, from the Gaiety Theatre, London. She was described as, 'the bright star around whom the minor satellites flutter and are made brighter by her extra brilliance' — AC.

'Patience', H.M.S. Pinafore (performed several times) and 'Iolanthe'. Pantomimes, too, were particularly enjoyed, such as 'Goody Two Shoes', 'Bluebeard', 'Jack the Giant Killer', 'Sinbad the Sailor', and 'The Babes in the Wood'.

Another well liked production was 'Uncle Tom's Cabin'. For more serious tastes, The National Grand Opera Company and Miss Alleyn and her Shakespearean Company consisting of twenty artistes appeared.

For lighter preferences, entertainment included the queen of burlesque, Nellie Farren, the Livermore Court Minstrels, the Christy Minstrels, and the Hague's Minstrels.

Also, for those who liked light music, there was the most popular, 'Les Cloches de Corneville', and, Offenbach's, 'La Fille du Tambour Major'.

Many well known companies came to Colchester — including Edgar Bruce's, Charles Hawtrey's and Auguste Creamer's. For less educated tastes, Colchester Theatre gave popular melodramas, such as 'Sweeney Todd', 'Black Eyed Susan', and, 'Maria Marten', or 'The Murder in the Red Barn'.

Amateur performers were usually well supported by Colcestrians. One amateur actor was to become famous in another sphere. BP — Baden Powell, the future originator of the Scouting Movement.

A Colchester character died on February 26th, 1881; James Hurnard, a brewer on East Hill, an ardent Liberal, and an Alderman. He was also a man of poetical efforts, chiefly a volume entitled, 'The Setting Sun'. He was a well-known Quaker, and resided latterly at Hill House, Lexden.

THE NINETIES

A feature of the Queen's birthday parade on May 24th, 1895 was the appearance of the boys from the South Metropolitan School, Witham.

Two years later Colchester celebrated the great Victoria's Diamond Jubilee. On that June day celebrations started at eleven o'clock in the morning when there was a cycle parade at Lexden Park. Cyclists rode through the town participating in a battle of flowers and confetti, and a number of prizes were offered.

At two o'clock a procession took place. This included the Mayor (James Paxman) and Corporation, members of several Friendly societies, several bands, the corporation fire brigade, the Celebration Committee, the Colchester Rowing Club (with their decorated and manned boats), etc. After passing through the High Street, Queen Street, St. Botolph's Street, to the Abbey Field, a square was formed. The bands played the National Anthem and the mayor declared open a free fête for the people. Athletic sports included climbing greasy poles. There was a steam circus and other forms of amusement such as a shooting gallery and aunt sallies. London artistes included Olenzo, the continental marvel, the Gigardo troupe of acrobats, Edward Mortimer, the lightning cartoonist, Mr. Fred Greville, a champion spade and stilt dancer, the Errados on the horizontal bar, the Bros. Loretti on the double trapeze, and the Alabama Coons. The evening brought a lantern cycle ride followed by a firework display and a huge bonfire. A little later in the year some seven thousand school children were entertained, and presented with a medal.

In July, 1893, the royal wedding of H.R.H. the Duke of York with the Princess Mary of Teck, had been celebrated by a 'monster tea and entertainment to the children, a military torchlight tattoo, an illuminated cycle ride, and fireworks'.

Primrose Day was still remembered in 1890 when 'all sorts and conditions of men, sported their button-hole', and 'the ladies were very much in evidence'.

In April, 1892, the Young Man's Christian Association opened new premises recently rented, at number 15, High Street. In the following January, a Mr. Eddy, of the Y.M.C.A. gave a view on late Victorian Colchester. He thought the different classes did not mingle well and Colcestrians were said to be of phlegmatic temperament, and lacking in hospitality. He stated they were not interested in politics, that

The re-opening of the Albert School of Art by Lord Rosebery K.G.K.T. on October 20th, 1896. In the Art section the list of subjects included painting and drawing in oils and water colours, modelling, carving, etc. — CM.

Trinity Street in 1888 by Nancy Fisher. It joins Culver Street and Sir Isaac's Walk. Formerly it was called Trinity Lane, and Scheregate Lane — EL.

the tradesmen were not very enterprising, and things were not so cheap.

Mr. Eddy was more complimentary about industry as Colchester was 'well ahead of the times and manufactures were progressing!' Recreation amusements, the park, recreation ground and clubs, 'went to make the town abreast with the times'. The theatre and music halls were conducted, 'with about as much morality as any'. Municipally, Mr. Eddy stated, the town was quite up to the times. It was a right step to adopt a school board to replace the so called voluntary system. Good work was being done in working towards a free library and by the School of Art.

Despite the town being a military centre, only two in a thousand of the population were drunk.

The population in 1891 was 34,559. The rise in population since 1841 was due to new industries, especially an engineering industry and also to the new military camp. The railway had been equally useful to both.

The population in the parishes in May, 1893, were as follows: All Saints 837, Holy Trinity 1,302, St. Botolph's

Holy Trinity Church in the eighteen eighties. A stained glass window, to the memory of Miss Corsellis, was placed in the east end of the church in 1851. The tower is Saxon — AC.

7,623, St. Giles 5,651, St. James 2,926, St. Leonard 2,918, St. Martin 957, St. Mary's at the Walls 3,327, St. Mary Magdalen 585, St. Michael's, Mile End, 1,082, St. Nicholas 873, St. Peter's 2,363, and St. Runwald 238.

The anniversary of Plassey Day was well kept in June, 1890, when the Royal Munster Fusiliers held their annual regimental sports.

There was a 'Field Day' at Middlewick in August four years later 'The various officers received orders which placed them in command of a certain number of men, with whom they had to attack a position or act as defenders. The field day, therefore, resolved itself into a series of small battles, cavalry, artillery, and infantry being employed in turn, and after some interesting manoeuvres, the troops marched back into camp'.

There were two military occasions in August, 1895. One was a grand combined concert by the band of XX Hussars, and the King's (Liverpool) Regiment, and a grand lantern display by the band, buglers, and others of the 1st. Volunteer Battalion Suffolk Regiment.

The other was a grand military display at Reed Hall. This included mounted and dismounted combats and displays, tent pegging, lemon cutting, sword versus lance, sword versus bayonet, physical drill, quarter staff, bayonet and gymnastic display, officers gymkhana races, maypole and quadrille drill. Three military bands were in attendance.

Colcestrians who feared that the garrison was in danger of diminishing were heartened in October, 1896, by the erection of a new Military Hospital. There was also some reconstruction in the Camp.

In August, two years later, large numbers of townspeople assembled at St. Botolph's Station to welcome the 2nd Royal Warwicks.

Salvation Army dinners for poor children were started in January, 1891, by Mr. William Nurse, the Captain of the Colchester detachment and others. A good dinner was assured to any child under ten, from any part of the borough, who presented itself at the Salvation Army Barracks. Children flocked to the feast, 'each carrying a basin or mug and spoon

The Military Hospital was built in 1896 — AC.

— for they are required to provide themselves with these'.

On May 9th, in the following year, General Booth again came to Colchester.

Due to the severe February weather in 1895, the Mayor (Mr. C. E. Egerton-Green) in conjunction with the Salvation Army took steps for a Soup Kitchen at the Salvation Army Barracks, St. John's Avenue.

A School Board started in the town in 1892. At that time there were 5,583 children of school age, of whom 695 did not attend school. 1,700 school places were needed and some buildings were no longer available.

In January, 1895, a sketch appeared in the 'Essex Standard' of the new Board Schools at North Street — 'the schools, apart from their perfect utility, are a distinct ornament to the town. The playgrounds cover in all two acres, and are divided into three portions — for boys, girls and infants'.

A year later, Barrack Street School, intended to accommodate 1,200 children, was opened.

On April 25th, 1896, the Corn Exchange was the scene of a remarkable gathering when, 'in recognition of the valuable work they perform', 'about 900 Sunday and Elementary schoolteachers were invited to a reception and entertainment 'by the Mayor and Mayoress (Alderman and Mrs. Wicks).

A concert was given in March, 1898, by children of St. Michael's Myland Day School. The elder scholars delivered 'with much animation' an action song, entitled, 'The Proud Pig'. 'Little Florrie Balls recited her griefs which centred on her sick doll and deservedly was encored'. 'Red Leaves', a glee, was sung by the school choir. The elder girls gave a fan drill dance and the elder scholars gave a scarf dance. Little Rosie Larter recited, 'To School for the first time', and 'Master A. Strowlger proved an adept in the art of photography'.

The Rev. S. Baring Gould, the famous author, preached at various services at All Saints, Stanway, in July, 1898, on behalf of the parish school. He referred to the importance of education, and said that the State System insisted that no child should be stinted in the opportunity of mental improvement. The state could not, however, provide any definite form of religious instruction for there were so many forms of religion'.

In October, 1892, there was a meeting to form a local branch of the National Society of Prevention of Cruelty to Children. This was a cause that certainly must have pleased Dr. Barnado who again visited Colchester on April 6th, 1897, when he spoke at the Corn Exchange about his work.

The juveniles still enjoyed celebrating Guy Fawkes Day. On that day in 1898, 'the "Town Guy" attired in theatrical costume paraded the streets mounted on anything but a fiery steed, and attended by the usual party of javelin men'. 'A few urchins wore a mask or bedaubed their faces with red ochre. Their clothes were adorned with paper frilling'.

Several antiques were discovered during this decade. In August, 1891, a fine specimen of a Roman horse shoe was found in Maidenburgh Street. In the following August, several large pieces of Roman paving were found at the rear of Mr. Locke's premises, in Queen Street. In the next month, finds at St. Botolph's corner, included a Roman silver coin.

There was a complaint in April, 1893, about damage done to the old Roman wall, at the bottom of Roman Road. The path was strewed with stones for yards, apparently pulled down by 'persons scrambling up and down the wall'.

In 1892 the Roman collection of the late Alderman Jarmin was acquired, and in September of the following year a 'Fairy Fête' with coloured lamps was held in aid of the Joslin Museum Fund. The concert was held on the Holly Trees lawn, and concluded with a grand firework display, and an ascent of fire balloons. The great Roman collection of Mr. George Joslin was bought through public subscription by the efforts of the Mayor, Mr. Gurney Benham. As the museum was now crowded, more space was needed.

The Early Closing Movement made more progress in this decade. In April, 1890, the Mayor issued a circular to the various millinery and dress making establishments in the borough, asking that the privilege of 2 o'clock closing on Thursdays, now so generally accorded to the shop assistants in Colchester, may be extended to the assistants in these establishments.

By June apparently everyone, including most tobacconists, closed on Thursday afternoon. The following year, in May, merchants and tradesmen unanimously decided to close at 2 p.m. on Thursdays from May to September (inclusive).

May 5th was the first day of the closing season in 1892. Nearly all shops closed their doors at 2 pm and Lieut. Col. Howard again very kindly offered his lawn on alternate Thursdays for tennis, croquet, etc.

In September an assistant suggested that all shops should be closed at seven o'clock in the winter months, or else at 4 o'clock one evening in the week.

By April, 1898, this movement felt they had achieved some success when all shops closed at 2 o'clock on one day of the week all the year round.

In postal affairs, on and after May 29th, 1892, a bag from London was received every Sunday morning, and the correspondence it contained fell into the Sunday delivery in the town and some of the rural districts. In June a wall letter box was erected in Stanwell Street. The Post Office opened trunk lines between Colchester and many of the most important towns. The Post Office was enlarged to three times its present area in 1897. Two houses, a stable and other buildings were demolished, and an entrance was allowed from Church Street North for mail carts.

Despite the Colchester Bank failure, that marred Christmas 1891. progress was made in the town in the nineties.

The 'Park' question came to the fore in June, 1890, when a movement suggested adapting the charming grounds of Lexden Park as a 'Public Park and Gardens for Colchester'. This would have been the upper portion of the park, comprising approximately sixty acres.

An important report was presented in April, 1892, pointing out that on November 9th of the previous year, the Corporation adopted a resolution approving of the land near the castle, belonging to the trustees of the late Mr. C. G. Round, as the best site for the proposed new park, to be established under the bequest of the late Mr. R. D. Catchpole.

Numerous daily visitors, in August, 1892, watched a large number of workmen preparing the Castle Park. The castle bailey and Sheepshead meadow became a rendezvous for promenading at leisure. The roadway to Sheepshead meadow was not yet completed. A road into the bailey at the back of the castle began and many were engaged in levelling and other work in the Sheepshead meadow. (Considerable progress was made with the help of the fine weather.) At the top of the meadow, the terrace intended for a bandstand and promenade was levelled and turfed. The old drain protected

The Lower Castle Park to be. This is how it looked in the eighteen eighties. In the centre is Choppings Mill. Originally Colchester had at least four mills — CM.

with brickwork, and the old wall that ran beneath the ramparts of the Holly Trees, could now easily be seen.

The park was officially opened on October 20th.

On a March Sunday in 1893, the lower park was thrown open to the public for the first time. The lake and several other important features were still unfinished.

Two months later, military bands played fortnightly on Thursday afternoons from 3.30-4.30. These bands played in different parts of the park to find out the best place for a bandstand.

In June, a handsome earthen plaque representing the castle as it appeared at the opening of the Castle Park, could be sent post free for 1s.9d from The Ancient House, 30 Head Street.

Messrs. Bloomfield & Co., St. Botolph's Street, in January, 1894, were to supply a new iron wire guard fence to protect the grass and flower beds in the Castle Park.

'The Essex Standard' for October 7th, 1892, included a small plan and sketch of the New Central Public Library with its Librarian's Rooms, Lending Library, Reference Library, Entrance Hall, Reading Room (50 ft. x 25 ft.), and the adjoining St. Runwald's churchyard.

In October, a year later, there appeared a sketch of the new public library in the same newspaper. The building was, 'on the whole admiredly adapted for the purposes for which it had been erected and fitted'. It was opened by the Lord High Chancellor, Lord Herschell, on the day of the Oyster

Feast, another guest being the Lord Mayor of London, Sir George Robert Tyler. High Street was particularly gay with bunting, but large banners, Union Jacks and Royal Standards, floated gaily from private and business establishments in the principal streets.

The directors of the New Corn Exchange, in January, 1894, added a 'most convenient room to their commanding premises'. Its size 42 ft. x 18 ft. 6 ins. was considered suitable to hire for such occasions as meetings, classes, evening parties, etc. The room could accommodate about a hundred and fifty, and had two approaches.

There was some restoration to St. Peter's Church, especially the roof, in 1894.

In September, 1892, a Grand Fête and Fancy Fair was held at Lexden Park for the restoration and enlargement of Lexden Church. Four years later, in March, Lexden Park was again open, on terms for promenading and cycling.

By Spring, 1890, there was an influenza epidemic. Several hundreds of men in the Colchester Camp and Barracks were laid up with it. A year later, in June, an outbreak of diphtheria was caused by defective drains in Charles Street. Several deaths in 1898 were due to diphtheria.

Details for mortality in Colchester Jan. 1st-23rd 1892, were as follows:

	Influenza	Bronchitis	Other Causes	Total
1st Ward	9	25	19a	53
2nd Ward	16	10	12b	38
3rd Ward	9	13	16c	38
Total	34	48	47	129

In this decade there were some very useful souvenirs to remind the visitor of the historic town. The latest novelty, in perfumery, in 1892, was 'Rozenia' or 'Colchester Rose Bouquet' — 'deliciously fragrant' with a 'delightfully pleasant and lasting odour'. The bottle and style were extremely elegant the label being a beautiful engraving in miniature of that 'interesting ruin, St. Botolph's Priory'.

Four years later it was possible to purchase Castle wool with a 'photograph of the grand old castle', from T. Alfred Dodd, 34 and 35 Long Wyre Street.

Electric lighting was installed for the first time in a private house in May, 1892. Mr. F. W. Friend introduced incandescent lighting throughout the whole of the millinery

The Fire Brigade. In 1842 it had three engines and a brigade of twenty men. In 1886 the volunteer brigade was taken over by the Corporation. The Corporation brigade was formed in 1896. This photograph is a few years later — CM.

premises, Alma House, High Street. The electric power came from Messrs. Sanders and Sons. The shop had nineteen lights and the rooms and passages of the private house had twelve lights. A powerful light was also attached to the outside wall at the back entrance.

Four years later the question of electric lighting in the town was reconsidered. The streets were still lighted with flat flame burners, and the outskirts with oil lamps.

The Council decided to construct an electricity works in 1897 and a general supply began on December 1st, 1898.

A new waterworks was constructed in 1894, and two years later a reliable and complete pumping plant was installed.

The Colchester Fire Brigade was formed in 1896. A horse-drawn steam fire engine was bought, and in September had its trial run.

'The Essex Standard' in February, 1893, published a sketch of the proposed new railway station. Three years later the new buildings were opened. The front presented 'a handsome appearance', and there was 'an excellent approach to it for vehicles, while there is a covered way so that people alighting from cabs, etc. are sheltered'.

The nineties brought popular cycling. On Good Friday, 1892, members of the Excelsior Cycling Club held their annual paper chase. 'The only accident happened through a dog getting in the machine, causing the cyclist to descend from his perch'.

Two years later, in August, an employee of the Standard Ironworks was, 'riding down North Hill with his feet on the rests, when a large rat ran out of the yard at the bottom of the hill. The rider was thrown but unhurt when it got entangled in the spokes of one of the wheels, but the rat was instantly killed'.

The Colchester Excelsior and Athletic Club held a Soirée Ball at the Drill Hall in January, 1895. At their ball in the following month, the hall was, 'nicely decorated, on the stage being an effective display of bicycles surrounded by ferns and foliage plants'.

Cyclists were in the local news in 1896. One collided with a cab, another knocked down a child. There was also a collision between cyclists. In September they were considered

The arrival of the first car in Colchester in about 1896. It is going up East Hill and creates much interest — CM.

The great actress, Ellen Terry came to Colchester in 1890 — AC.

a danger if they rode full speed down North Hill. Thirty cycles were sold in one lot to the Regimental Cycling Club of the King's (Liverpool) Regiment. Colcestrians were concerned with the wheeling of the bicycles and perambulators on the footpaths.

The cab was the Victorian equivalent of the modern taxi. In the nineties cab and omnibus drivers received substantial Christmas boxes and were entertained at the Cups Hotel through the kindness of Mr. and Mrs. Mackenzie.

Much interest was caused in the High Street one July day, 1896, when a 'horseless carriage' was seen on its journey from London to a village fête at Great Bentley. It was to do sixty miles in three hours. A special permit had to be allowed for as yet such vehicles were not legal. After taking in fuel it 'proceeded at a smart pace down East Hill'. On March 27th of the following year, a sensation was caused by the sudden appearance of a motor car. It was something like a waggonete in shape, and several gentlemen, 'took short trips and pronounced the sensation agreeable as well as novel'.

The lease of the Theatre Royal was taken over by the newly formed Colchester Theatre Company Limited, in 1889.

In April, 1890, Miss Ellen Terry was the attraction at Mr. Clark's Annual Matinée at the theatre. She received 'quite an ovation' and recited, 'In the Round Tower of Jhansi — June 1857' by Christina Rossetti. She read with such feeling that even Miss Terry herself was 'visibly moved'. She also gave, 'The Vulgar Little Boy' from 'The Ingoldsby Legends' which brought much amusement. She also recited, 'The Whistle' charmingly.

Charles Macdona acquired the theatre in 1892. The building in the April of that year, resounded with the current hit, 'Ta-ra-ra-boom-de-ay'.

In the same month, Madame Antoinette Sterling, the leading contralto of the nineties, entertained.

'Robinson Crusoe' was the pantomime in January 1894, the title role being taken by Miss Rose Smith. A chorus of children also recieved much applause. Of the specialities brought into the wedding scene, 'perhaps the dance by little Rosie Leaf made the best impression'. There was also a clever contortion by the 'human corkscrew', and a statue ballad by four young ladies was re-demanded. A burst of enthusiasm welcomed the Transformation Scene, 'The Home of Britannia'.

Five months later, Professor Crocker's 'educated' horses, ponies, mules and donkeys (numbering thirty altogether), came to the theatre, 'They play at school, at leap frog, hold a solemn court of justice, ring bells singly and in concert, take a citadel by siege, and a number of equally extraordinary things'.

Mr. Martin Harvey was the son of a Wivenhoe celebrity. He acted in Colchester in 1895 and later. He was knighted — AC.

Ben Greet's Company appeared in January, 1895, in 'A Midsummer Night's Dream'. The production included four ballets, the ballet of flowers and of the bees, the shadow ballet, and the electric ballet.

In April that year, Miss Clara Butt, the much talked of contralto sang at Mr. Clark's Matinée Musicale.

Of plays that have lasted up to the present, audiences saw Wilde's 'A Woman of No Importance', in which 'The plot is the least important feature of the play', 'The Second Mrs. Tanqueray', 'Charley's Aunt', and Barrie's, 'The Little Minister'.

'Under the Czar', a melodrama, received tremendous applause with the line, 'A pretty girl never appealed to a British soldier in vain'.

Mr. John Martin Harvey, son of a local celebrity of Wivenhoe, appeared in August, 1895, with a company from the Lyceum Theatre. He acted as Rouget de L'Isle in 'An Old Song', and Eba Jakia in 'King Rene's Daughter'.

On one Saturday afternoon in April 1893, a novel entertainment was given by children at the Public Hall. Master Slaughter, aged eight, played a pianoforte solo, as well as the accompaniments. Miss Maud Slaughter, also aged eight, sang three songs nicely. Masters Willie and Henry Richards, aged nine and thirteen, played violin solos and a duet, and Miss Eva Nevard recited, 'very intelligently'.

In December of the following year, Miss Ruby Hughes held an 'At Home' at the Red Lion Assembly Room. The children danced the Barn Dance, the Tambourine Dance, the Skirt Dance, the Cachuca, etc.

The Juvenile Marshall's Minstrels, a group comprising of seventeen youngsters, came in 1898. The entertainment included a comic song by Master Toby Cooper, aged about 10, a pretty song and dance act by Miss Daisy Howard, and dances by the Eugene Quartette.

On an April Wednesday evening in 1892, there was on display at the theatre, 'the greatest marvel of the age, the wonderful 'Talking Machine', Edison's latest phonograph exhibited and described by Mr. William Lynd, the lecturer especially appointed to represent the illustrious American inventor, Thomas Alva Edison'.

Mr. Albert Chevalier sang some of his popular numbers at the Corn Exchange on Whit Monday, 1896. These included, 'The future Mrs. 'Awkins', 'Wot Cher or Knocked-em in the Old Kent Road', and 'My Old Dutch'.

In the same year Colcestrians could hear Mr. Tridar Nachez, the celebrated Hungarian violinist.

In the nineties the town had its own child genius, pianist, Miss Muriel Mustard, a frail figure who had the honour of playing to the great Hummel and M. Vladimir de Pachmann, as well as to aristocratic families.

For six days at the Corn Exchange in October, 1896, there was a unique entertainment for the first time in the town of the, 'living photographs' — prophetic of the cinema and the twentieth century.

The programme then included, 'Hampstead Heath on Bank Holiday, Arrival of an Express Train, Persimmon wins the Derby, Engineer at work on Nelson Docks, Scene on Blackfriars Bridge, Traffic near the Houses of Parliament, Struggle with a betting man and police, Brighton Beach, Comic Costume Race at Sports, Royal Wedding, Up the River, Trilby, etc.'

For two nights at the Corn Exchange in February 1898, David Devants 'Animated Photographs, direct from Maskelyne and Cooke, Egyptian Hall, London, reproduced by the cinematograph, could be witnessed. There were between thirty and forty entertaining and exciting and humorous scenes, including the Queen's Diamond Jubilee Procession, with all the movements of real life. These were interspersed with original musical sketches by Mr. Griffith Humphreys, Society Entertainer'.

Colcestrians still visited the circus. In September, 1893, Lord George Sanger's Circus included, 'lady acrobats, a ladder fiend, a comic mule, Herr Ulric's barrel evolution, the trapeze performance, and the "fire horse" which rescued a dummy baby from a burning house'.

A unique 'Carnival on Ice' was held on Mr. Spalding's field near North Bridge, on Wednesday, February 13th, 1895. A large number of 'gaily and variously attired skaters attended'. There were impersonations of the borough's Conservative and Liberal candidates, firemen, Japanese warriors, witches, hospital nurses, pierrots and clowns, Britannia and Renshaw with his tennis racket, and Girton girls. 'Mephistopheles freely mingled, while a "policeman" facetiously kept order'.

Crouch Street, early 1900's. It joins Headgate and Lexden Road. To the right can be seen Charles E. Rice, greengrocer, and to the left, Moore & Sons, grocers. If the scheme that Sir Samuel Morton Peto nursed through the 1850's had succeeded, a railway line would have ended here — EL.

EPILOGUE

On October 31st, 1898, H.R.H. the Duke of Cambridge, laid the foundation stone of the new Town Hall, the architect of this municipal venture being Mr. John Belcher, F.R.I.B.A. The old Town Hall, like the century and the Victorian Age itself, was moving to its close. Its demolition had started by January, 1899. 'The internal fittings were removed and as far as possible adapted to the use of the temporary Law Courts and offices, and on a Tuesday the work of demolishing the fabric commenced. Men were engaged on stripping the roof and also in erecting a palisading around the building. On the Wednesday the upper portion of the structure was attacked and gradually disappeared. Many people watched the removal of the balustrode facing High Street, and on the following day a considerable crowd watched the removal of larger corner stones, which, after being loosened, were pitched bodily down into the enclosure round the hall, and in several cases were deeply embedded in the earth'.

'The Municipal Journal' showed a frontispiece of the new Town Hall, and described as being erected, 'one of the finest Town Halls in the country. No town of the same size will have such municipal buildings.' The estimated cost was nearly £36,000.

The report continued, 'The best feature is the tower, which has enabled Mr. Belcher to finish the building in a way worthy of his style'.

Miss Edna May came to Colchester in 1899 — AC.

The building was to be built on the lines of the later Renaissance style.

One of the 'stars' at Mr. Clark's Matinée Musicale in 1899 was Miss Edna May, described as, 'not only a very beautiful young lady but she possesses a very pure and charming voice'. She sang her Salvation song from 'The Belle of New York'. She was presented with a basket of flowers, as was another artiste, Miss Louie Pounds, 'who sang very pleasantly, Slaughter's "Whisper my name in the Twilight".'

Barnum and Bailey's Great Show descended on Drury Farm and performed on July 24th, 1899. It was all on a gigantic scale. A dozen pavilions seated nearly 15,000 persons. There were so many performers that the programme was bewildering. These included, 'new human curiosities and prodigies, freak animals and new rare, wild beasts. There were three rings, two stages, a race track, and great aerial enclive'.

By the end of 1899 soldiers from Colchester were participating in the Boer War. In November, Miss Chadwick, superintendent of the Garrison Hospital, left to take charge of the Prince of Wales hospital ship.

At the beginning of 1900, The New Town Hall Pamphlet was published by Messrs. Benham and Co., and gave, 'interesting details and beautifully executed illustrations'.

Later in the year, the new Town Hall was considered a repository of county objects of interest and importance, local art, local antiquities, etc. The figure of St. Helena, in December, was fixed on the Victoria Tower.

Highlights at the Theatre Royal included the D'Oyly Carte Company in 'The Mikado', and 'The Rose of Persia', Mr. Harry Paulton's Company in the comedy, 'Niobe', 'The Sign of the Cross', and Miss Letty Lind who sang and danced, 'La Fragesca' one September Friday evening.

Mr. Charles Macdona announced that the theatre was to have improved electric lighting, new heating apparatus, a large dress circle and a spacious pit.

Letty Lind came to Colchester in 1900 — AC.

The pantomime, 'Aladdin', included many patriotic songs and allusions to the doings of the 'Soldiers of the Queen' in South Africa. 'A good percentage of the troops of Lord Alwyne's Horse Regiment in the audience joined in many choruses of the warlike songs'.

One April evening Mrs. Goslin gave an interesting lecture at the Soldiers Home, Queen Street, on the work of the South African General Mission. She mentioned that this was the only mission doing work amongst the soldiers.

May brought the procession to celebrate the relief of Mafeking which was soon followed by the loyal town celebrating the Queen's eighty first birthday. 'In many conspicuous places portraits of Her Majesty supplanted those of the hero of the hour, draped in the national colours or garlanded with flowers'. Button portraits and coloured favours were also generally worn, the cabbie whips and steeds were bedecked,

FRANC
CORN & SEED
ESTHER

and the bells of St. Peter's rang throughout the day. 'Later there was a fine military parade on the Abbey Field despite none of the regular troops taking part'.

On Whit Monday and Whit Tuesday, 'animated pictures' of the War were shown at the Corn Exchange, 'a splendid photo, of Lord Roberts met with an enthusiastic reception so did the one which illustrated Mr. Kruger leaving the Volksraad. The climax was reached, however, when a magnificent portrait of Her Majesty was shown upon the screen'.

Also at the Corn Exchange, on one July Thursday, Mr. Frederic Villiers, the well known war artist of 'The Illustrated London News', gave a very interesting lecture on the South African War, entitled, 'Kruger and Khaki'.

On Thursday evenings in the same month, military bands played at the Abbey field from eight o'clock until ten o'clock. On one occasion, 'as it grew dark some Chinese lanterns were lit, and the scene rendered was very picturesque'. Later in the year there was Sunday Military Band Music at the Cavalry Barracks.

Military Road 1899. The large house in the photograph has not been identified. This was another unfashionable part of town. In 1879 the New Town was built in this area and the Military Road included Camp Church, Groom, Daniells & Co. were timber and slate merchants, and J. Leech owned the Royal Mortar Inn — EL.

Left:
The Hythe at the turn of the century — AC.

General Booth spoke three times at the Rink on one September Sunday.

Colcestrians had musical treats this year by listening to the Blue Hungarian Band, and Miss Clarabel Hyde.

A tourist to the town in October commented upon 'the tall elms and rolling meadows of Lexden, the western suburbs with trim-built villas bordering the road, and the town centre with its quaint and busy streets on either hand and Jumbo (the water tower), "brutally dominating everything" and looking, "very big, very ugly, and very prominent" '.

On the first of December, Mr. John Everitt, the Town Crier, paraded the streets, and finished by saying, 'God bless Tommy Atkins, the absent minded beggar fighting in South Africa, a merry Christmas to you all, God Save the Queen'.

The Queen died on January 22nd, 1901. The Mayor, Claude Egerton-Green's request for Colcestrians to go into mourning and for private houses to have shutters pulled up or blinds drawn was responded to quickly. A muffled peal of bells was rung at St. Peter's, and the bells of St. Nicholas, All Saints, Holy Trinity and other churches were tolled.

At the theatre, Mr Macdona returned the money to those who had paid for admission, and closed for that and the following evening.

Lexden in the eighteen sixties. By this time the Lexden Road had become a fashionable promenade instead of a country road. Note the blacksmith's, William Hutley, Church House and the water splash. The Rev. John Papillon lived at the rectory, George Henry Errington at Lexden Park nearby. The Sun Inn was owned by Garrad Isaac Beardwell — AC.

West Stockwell Street in the late 19th, century. The first municpal library in 1894 was at the corner of West Stockwell Street and High Street. It is part of the Dutch Quarter when Flemings lived here. It has some good houses dating back to the Middle Ages — EL.

At the American Biograph (exhibited at the Corn Exchange), the entertainment was considerably shortened. The programme concluded with the last portrait taken of the Queen.

On the Wednesday flags were displayed half mast at the temporary municipal buildings, on most of the church towers, at the Conservative Club, the Liberal Club, School of Art, and other buildings. Shutters or black boards were put up at nearly all business establishments. The police wore a band of crape round the left arm.

The Editorial of 'The Essex County Standard' for January 26th, 1901, expressed the feeling of the time in the following words:

'Her subjects can hardly realise in a moment that the Victorian Era, the era of such grand strides of progress in all that is humanising and promotive of civilisation, is at a finished cycle'.

A new chapter of history had begun.

ACKNOWLEDGEMENTS

I would like to acknowledge the help given me by Mr. D. T-D. Clarke, Curator of the Colchester and Essex Castle Museum.

Also I would like to thank the staff of the Essex Libraries Local Studies Dept. Colchester central library for help with illustrations.

I am also grateful to the staff of the former central library for providing me with the old newspapers from which to glean much interesting and useful information.

Lastly, I should like to thank all those people who have shown interest and given me encouragement with this project.

Bibliography, etc.

Essex Standard 1837-1879, 1886-1901.

Essex Telegraph 1880-1885.

A book entitled Centenary of the Municipal Corporation Act, issued by Colchester Town Council, January 1936.

Official Illustrated Guide to the Great Eastern Railway by George Measom.

The Story of Colchester by Geoffrey Martin.

Colchester Worthies by C. E. Benham.

Article: Colchester's Hythe in days gone by. G. W. Martin.

Article: The Theatre Royal, Colchester, by Gerald O. Rickword.

Articles in Supplement Coronation year. Essex County Standard. 1937.

The Street Names of Colchester, by Alderman E. Alec Blaxill JP.

Directory 1855 and Kelly's Directory for 1862, 1870 and 1888.

Cullingford's Annual and Colchester Guide for 1895.

Notes on Illustrations

AC stands for photographs or postcards from the author's collection.

CM stands for photographs from the Colchester Castle Museum Collection. By courtesy.

EL stands for photographs from the Essex Libraries Local Studies Dept. Colchester Collection. By courtesy.

Some are taken by the National Monuments Record, Fortress House, Saville Row, London, W1. for which permission has been given.

INDEX